ENDpapers Fourte

KU-694-022

International Terrorism and International Law

Incorporating the END Bulletin of the Bertrand Russell Peace Foundation and the Spokesman
Edited by Ken Coates

Spokesman 52   Winter 1986-87   £3.95

CONTENTS

Copyright © *Spokesman* 1987

Printed by the Russell Press Ltd., Nottingham, UK

ISSN 0262 7922   ISBN 0 85124 461 0

**Subscriptions
(3 issues)**
Institutions £16.00
Individual £9.00
USA:
Institutions $35
Individuals $20
Earlier volumes in the series available at £3.95 each

Published by the
Bertrand Russell Peace
Foundation Ltd.,
Bertrand Russell House
Gamble Street
Nottingham NG7 4ET
England
Tel. (0)602 784504

2

Editorial

After Reykjavik

The collapse of the Reykjavik summit meeting was felt nowhere more keenly than in Europe, the most heavily militarized continent in the world. Europeans have no reason to go to war with one another, but the division of their region into blocs has brought with it the deployment of nuclear arsenals, and the danger that conflict might spill back into the European region from any one of numerous "hot spots" around the world. In Iceland the two great power leaders negotiated alone. There was no European presence in their talks, even though the future of our continent was one of the chips on the bargaining table.

President Reagan and General Secretary Gorbachev seemed to be close to agreement on the removal of all the so-called intermediate nuclear weapons in Europe. A wide ranging agreement on strategic weapons was also within reach. Both these substantial advances were stalemated however, by the President's continued refusal to negotiate about the Strategic Defence Initiative (popularly known as "Star Wars"). The overwhelming majority of Europeans, and certainly the peace movements of Europe must seek for ways to break this deadlock, which threatens all our futures.

The European Nuclear Disarmament Conventions share the ultimate goal of the removal of all nuclear weapons from our continent. Beyond doubt, the proposed Reykjavik agreement would have been a significant step in this direction. It is clear that such a step forward would be in the interests of everyone concerned, and is supportable in its own right, without any wider linkages. Peace movements all around the world will also agree that the Reykjavik proposals concerning strategic nuclear weapons should be implemented, and that the dangerous and deceptive "Star Wars" initiative should be stopped.

At the Sixth European Nuclear Disarmament Convention, in Coventry in July 1987, the European movements will explore the possibilities of co-operation on these issues, at the same time that they seek support from the American and Soviet peoples in opposing the SDI, and disconnecting any linkage which might hinder progress to agreed disarmament in Europe.

4

Within this framework, the Convention will consider three main topics: What are the prospects for a new detente? How do the goals of European security fit with the process of disarmament? And how can the influence of the peace movements be extended to bring about effective action?

We shall see, in Coventry, that recent obituaries of the European Peace Movement are premature. Such movements are more necessary than ever they were.

Libya in US Demonology

Noam Chomsky

Noam Chomsky is Professor of Linguistics at the Massachusetts Institute of Technology. This paper was first published in the Covert Action Information Bulletin. *Spokesman has recently published a paper given by Noam Chomsky in Madrid at a conference organised by Professor Manuel Garrido, under the title* The Race to Destruction: Its Rational Basis *(Spokesman Pamphlet No.85, price £1).*

What is Terrorism?

St. Augustine tells the story of a pirate captured by Alexander the Great, who asked him "how he dares molest the sea?". "How dare you molest the whole world?" the pirate replied: "because I do it with a little ship only, I am called a thief; you, doing it with a great navy, are called an Emperor."

The pirate's answer was "elegant and excellent," St. Augustine relates. It captures with some accuracy the current relations between the United States and Libya, a minor actor on the stage of international terrorism.

More generally, St. Augustine's tale reaches to the heart of the cynical frenzy over "international terrorism" currently being orchestrated as a cover for Western violence, and illuminates the meaning of the concept in contemporary Western usage. The term "terrorism" came into use at the end of the 18th century, primarily to refer to violent acts of governments designed to ensure popular submission. That concept, plainly, is of little benefit to the practitioners of state terrorism, who, holding power, are in a position to control the system of thought and expression. The original sense has therefore been abandoned, and the term "terrorism" has come to be applied mainly to "retail terrorism" by individuals or groups.[1] Whereas the term was once applied to Emperors who molest their own subjects and the world, now it is restricted to thieves who molest the powerful.

Extricating ourselves from the system of indoctrination, we will use the term "terrorism" to refer to the threat or use of violence to intimidate or coerce (generally for political ends), whether it is the wholesale terrorism of the Emperor or the retail terrorism of the thief.

In the true sense of the term, Libya is a terrorist state: the latest Amnesty International Report lists the killings of 14 Libyan citizens by this terrorist state, four abroad, during 1985, the major acts of terrorism plausibly attributed to Libya. In the course of the hysteria orchestrated to serve other ends, all sorts of charges have been made, but the record confirms the April 1986 statement of a senior US intelligence official that "what happened a few weeks ago is that Qaddafi, who previously had used his people primarily to assassinate Libyan dissidents, made a clear decision to target Americans."[2] Qaddafi's alleged decision followed the Gulf of Sidra incident, when a US air and naval armada sank Libyan vessels with many killed, and is entirely legitimate, indeed much belated, under the cynical doctrines professed by the United States executive, as we shall see directly.

Amnesty International reports that Libya's terrorist killings began in early 1980, at the time when Jimmy Carter launched the terrorist war in El Salvador with Jose Napoleon Duarte serving as a cover to ensure that arms would flow to the killers. While Libya was killing 14 of its own citizens, along with a handful of others, the US client regime of El Salvador killed some 50,000 of its citizens in the course of what Bishop Rivera Y Damas, who succeeded the assassinated Archbishop Romero, described in October 1980 as "a war of extermination and genocide against a defenceless civilian population." The security forces who perform these necessary chores were hailed by Duarte, a few weeks later, for their "valiant service alongside the people against subversion" while he conceded that "the masses were with the guerrillas" when this exercise began under the Carter-Duarte alliance. Duarte expressed this praise for the mass murderers as he was sworn in as President of the Junta in an effort to lend it legitimacy and ensure the flow of arms after the murder of four American churchwomen. This was generally regarded in the USA as improper, though such partisans of terror and torture as Jeane Kirkpatrick and Alexander Haig, offered justification even for this act.

The slaughter in El Salvador is not mere state terrorism on a massive scale, but international terrorism, given the organization, supply, training and direct participation by the ruler of the hemisphere. The same is true of the massacre of some 70,000 Guatemalans in the same years, when US arms to the murderers flowed at close to the normal level contrary to what is commonly alleged, though it was necessary to call in US proxies, the neo-Nazi Argentine generals and Israel, to implement the slaughter more efficiently, and to construct an arms pipeline involving Belgium and other collaborators, under the illegal direction of the Pentagon and the CIA. Meanwhile Reagan and his associates extolled the killers and torturers for their human rights improvements and "total dedication to democracy." "The striking feature of Libyan atrocities," two observers note in reviewing the Amnesty International study of state terror, "is that they are the only ones whose numbers are sufficiently limited that the individual cases can be enumerated," in striking contrast to Argentina, Indonesia, or the Central American states where the Emperor molests the world.[3]

US international terrorism in El Salvador is hailed as a magnificent achievement across the mainstream political spectrum in the United States because it laid the basis of what is called "democracy" in Western parlance:

namely, the rule of elite groups serving the needs of the Global Enforcer with the public role reduced to an occasional ratification of elite decisions. In El Salvador, the United States organized what Herman and Brodhead call "demonstration elections" to pacify the home front, carried out in an atmosphere of "terror and despair, macabre rumour and grisly reality," in the words of the observers of the British Parliamentary Human Rights Group, while the US press lauded this demonstration of our passionate commitment to democracy, as *Pravda* perhaps also does under similar circumstances.[4] Guatemala is also considered a success, for similar reasons. When half the population is marched to the polls after it has been properly traumatized by US-backed violence, enlightened American humanists are overjoyed at this renewed demonstration of our love for democracy, untroubled by the rise in death squad killings after the elections (including at least 94 deaths and 35 disappearances in the weeks following the President's January inauguration), the open recognition by the newly-elected President that he can do nothing given the roots of actual power in the military and the oligarchy and that the civilian government are merely "the managers of bankruptcy and misery,"[5] and the fact that the reaction in the United States helps convert the elections into a means for the US to participate more fully in state terror and repression, as in El Salvador. In fact, elections in US terror states are often a disaster for the domestic population, for this essential reason. These two examples, of course, represent only a small part of the US role in international terrorism during the 1980s, and the grisly record goes back many years.

In short, Libya is indeed a terrorist state, but in the world of international terrorism, it is hardly even a bit player.

Whose Terrorism?

The pirate's maxim explains the useful concept of "international terrorism" only in part. It is necessary to add a second feature: an act of terrorism enters the canon only if it is committed by "their side," not ours. Consider, for example, the PR campaign about "international terrorism" launched in early 1981 by the Reagan Administration. The major text was Claire Sterling's *The Terror Network*, which offered an ingenious proof that international terrorism is a "Soviet-inspired" instrument "aimed at the destabilization of Western democratic society." The proof is that the major terrorist actions are confined to the Western democratic states, and are not "directed against the Soviet Union or any of its satellites or client states." This profound insight much impressed other terrorologists, notably, Walter Laqueur, who wrote that Sterling had provided "ample evidence" that terrorism occurs "almost exclusively in democratic or relatively democratic countries."[6]

The Sterling thesis is true, in fact true by definition, given the way the term "terrorism" is employed by the Emperor and his loyal coterie. Since only acts committed by "their side" count as terrorism, it follows that Sterling is necessarily correct, whatever the facts. In the real world, the story is quite different. The major victims of international terrorism[7] in the several decades prior to the Sterling-Laqueur pronouncements were Cuba and the

Palestinians, but none of this counts, by definition. When Israel bombs Palestinian refugee camps killing many civilians — often without even a pretence of "reprisal" — or sends its troops into Lebanese villages in "counter-terror" operations where they murder and destroy, or hijacks ships and places thousands of hostages in prison camps under horrifying conditions, this is not "terrorism"; in fact, the rare voices of protest are thunderously condemned by loyal Party Liners for their "anti-Semitism" and "double standard," demonstrated by their failure to join the chorus of praise for "a country that cares for human life" (*Washington Post*), whose "high moral purpose" (*Time*) is the object of never-ending awe and acclaim, a country which, according to its American claque, "is held to a higher law, as interpreted for it by journalists" (Walter Goodman).[8]

Similarly, it is not terrorism when paramilitary forces operating from US bases and trained by the CIA, bombard Cuban hotels, sink fishing boats and attack Russian ships in Cuban harbours, poison crops and livestock, attempt to assassinate Castro, and so on, in missions that were running almost weekly at their peak.[9] These and innumerable similar actions on the part of the Emperor and his clients are not the subjects of conferences and learned tomes, nor of anguished commentary and diatribes in the media and journals of opinion.

Not only is "terrorism" defined for ideological serviceability, but standards of evidence are also conveniently set so as to achieve the Emperor's goals. To demonstrate Libya's role as a state terrorist, the flimsiest evidence, or none at all, will suffice. The headline of a *New York Times* editorial justifying the terrorist attack that killed some 100 people in Libya reads "To Save the Next Natasha Simpson," referring to the 11-year-old American girl who was one of the victims of the terrorist attacks in the Rome and Vienna air terminals on 27th December, 1985; these victims entitle us to bomb Libyan cities "to discourage state-supported terrorism," the editors solemnly inform us. It is only a minor defect that no evidence has been presented to implicate Libya in these actions. The Italian and Austrian governments stated that the terrorists were trained in Syrian-controlled areas of Lebanon and had come via Damascus, a conclusion reiterated by Israeli Defence Minister Rabin. Four months later, in response to US claims about Libyan involvement in the Vienna attack, the Austrian Minister of the Interior stated that "there is not the slightest evidence to implicate Libya," again citing Syria as the connection and adding that Washington had never presented the evidence of Libyan complicity it had promised to provide to the Austrian authorities. He also added the correct but — in the US — inexpressible comment that the problem of Lebanese-based terrorism lies largely in the failure to solve the Palestine problem, which has led desperate people to turn to violence, exactly the result intended by US-Israeli terrorism, a matter to which we return.[10]

If an individual implicated in a terrorist act once paid a visit to Libya, or is alleged to have received training or funds from Libya in the past, that suffices for condemnation of Qaddafi as a "mad dog" who must be eradicated. The same standards would implicate the CIA in the murderous exploits of Cuban exiles, among numerous others. Keeping just to 1985, one of the suspects in the bombing of the Air India jumbo jet off Ireland that was the year's worst terrorist act, killing 329 people, was trained in an anti-communist school for mercenaries in Alabama. The terrorist action that cost the most lives in the Middle East was a car-bombing in Beirut in March 1986 that killed 80 people and wounded 200, carried out by a Lebanese intelligence unit trained and supported by the CIA, in an effort to kill a Shi'ite leader who was believed to have been involved in "terrorist attacks against US installations" in Beirut; the term "terrorism" is commonly used by foreign armies in reference to actions against them by the local population which, as in this case, plausibly sees them as an occupying force attempting to impose a detested political settlement.[11] By the standards of evidence used in the case of Libya, the US is the world's leading terrorist power, even if we exclude the wholesale terrorism ruled ineligible by the propaganda system by the means already described.

Reagan's Policy and the Evil Empire
What the President calls "the evil scourge of terrorism" (in the specific Western sense) was placed in the central focus of attention by the Reagan Administration when it came into office in 1981. The reasons were transparent, though inexpressible within the doctrinal system. The Administration was committed to three related policies, all achieved with some success: (1) transfer of resources from the poor to the rich; (2) a massive increase in the state sector of the economy in the traditional American way, through the Pentagon system, a device to force the public to invest in high technology industry by means of the state-guaranteed market for the production of high technology waste (armaments) and thus to contribute to the general programme of public subsidy, private profit, called "free enterprise"; and (3) a substantial increase in the US role in intervention, subversion, and international terrorism (in the true sense of the expression). Such policies cannot be presented to the public in the terms in which they are intended. They can be implemented only if the general population is properly frightened by monsters against whom we must defend ourselves.

The standard device is an appeal to the threat of what the President called "the monolithic and ruthless conspiracy" bent on world conquest — President Kennedy in this case, as he launched a rather similar programme[12] — Reagan's "Evil Empire". But confrontation with the Evil Empire can be a dangerous affair, so it is preferable to do battle with safer enemies designated as the Evil Empire's proxies, a choice that conforms well to the third plank in the Reagan agenda, pursued for quite independent reasons: to ensure "stability" and "order" in our global domains. The "international terrorism" of properly chosen pirates, or of enemies such as Nicaragua or Salvadorean peasants who dare to defend themselves from our terrorist attack, is a far preferable target, and with an efficiently functioning propaganda system, it can be exploited to induce a proper sense of fear and mobilization among the domestic population.

Libya fits the need perfectly. Qaddafi is easy to hate, and Libya is weak and defenceless so that martial flourishes and, when needed, murder of Libyans can be conducted with impunity. The glorious military victory in Grenada, a culmination of the extreme hostility and aggressiveness of the Carter-Reagan Administrations after the Bishop Government threatened to consider the needs of the poor population, served similar ends. The point is readily perceived abroad. American journalist Donald Neff, writing in a British publication about the March 1986 Gulf of Sidra incident, comments that "this was less of a Rambo-style operation than a demonstration of the bully on the block picking a fight. It was typical of Reagan. In his five years in office, he has repeatedly got away with lording it over little guys. He did this time too."[13] It is an interesting fact about American culture that this regular show of cowardice and two-bit thuggery seems to strike a responsive chord.

The PR specialists of the Reagan Administration understood the utility of the Libyan enemy and wasted little time in confronting this dangerous foe. Libya was at once designated as a prime agent of the Soviet-inspired "terror network," and in July 1981, a CIA plan to overthrow and possibly kill Qaddafi with a paramilitary campaign of terror within Libya was leaked to the press.[14]

We might note parenthetically that by US standards, this plan authorized Qaddafi to carry out acts of terror against American targets in "self-defence against future attack," the words of White House spokesman Larry Speakes presenting the official justification for the bombing of Tripoli and Benghazi. The same justification was reiterated at the United Nations by Vernon Walters and Herbert Okun. The Administration even had the gall to argue that this right, which not even Hitler claimed and which, if proclaimed by other violent states, would tear to shreds what little remains of global order and international law, is in accord with the United Nations Charter; no form of legal sophistry can bridge that gap, but Reagan's pronouncement was duly acclaimed by Anthony Lewis for its reliance "on a legal argument that violence against the perpetrators of repeated violence is justified as an act of self-defence." The reason why the US justified the attack "on the basis of pre-empting an attack, which could be seen as a form of self-defence, (rather) than as a retaliatory action" was explained by a State Department official, who noted that the UN Charter expressly forbids the use of force except in self-defence — in fact, self-defence against armed attack, until the UN acts after a formal request by the country that regards itself as the victim of a sudden and overwhelming armed attack.[15]

In August 1981, the anti-Qaddafi message "was reinforced by the trap laid for Libya in the Gulf of Sidra," a trap "elaborately planned on the US side" with the intent of a confrontation in which Libyan jets could be shot down, as they were, Edward Haley observes in his bitterly anti-Qaddafi study of US relations with Libya. One specific purpose, Haley plausibly argues, was to "exploit the 'Libyan menace' in order to win support for steps (the Administration) wished to take in pursuit of Secretary Haig's 'strategic consensus' against the Soviet Union, and as an element in the arrangements necessary for the creation of a Rapid Deployment Force," targeted primarily at the Middle East. In November, the Administration concocted a ludicrous tale about Libyan hit-men roaming the streets of Washington to assassinate Our Leader, eliciting feverish media commentary along with some limited scepticism. When questioned about the plot, Reagan stated: "We have the evidence, and (Qaddafi) knows it."[16] The story faded away when its purpose was served, and the press was sufficiently disciplined not to report the exposure in the British press that the "assassins" on the official US list, leaked in England, were prominent members of the (passionately anti-Libyan) Lebanese Amal, including Nabih Berri and the elderly religious leader of the Shi'ite community.[17]

Other tales included a Libyan threat to invade the Sudan across 600 miles of desert (with the Egyptian and US air forces helpless to impede this outrage) and a plot to overthrow the government of the Sudan in February 1983 — conveniently discovered at a moment when the Administration's reactionary constituency was charging it with insufficient militancy, a plot so subtle that the Sudanese and Egyptian intelligence knew nothing about it as US reporters who took the trouble to go to Khartoum to investigate quickly discovered. The US responded to the fabricated plot with an elaborate show of force, enabling Secretary of State Shultz, who had been denounced as too faint-hearted, to strike heroic poses on television while announcing that Qaddafi "is back in his box where he belongs" because Reagan acted "quickly and decisively" against this threat to world order. Again, the episode was forgotten when its purposes had been served. There has been a series of similar examples. The media have generally played their appointed role, with only occasional demurrers.[18]

Gulf of Sidra Provocation

The events of March-April 1986 fit the familiar pattern to perfection. The Gulf of Sidra operation in March was plainly timed to stir up jingoist hysteria just prior to the crucial Senate vote on contra aid, coinciding with a fabricated Nicaraguan "invasion" of Honduras as Nicaragua exercised its legal right of hot pursuit to expel from its territory US proxy forces dispatched by their master from their Honduras bases to sow terror in Nicaragua prior to the Senate vote. The PR campaign succeeded brilliantly as demonstrated by the enraged reaction of Congressional doves and the media fairly generally, and the Senate vote. The charade also permitted the Administration to provide $20 million of military aid to Honduras, which Honduras officially maintains that it did not request, and which has no doubt been conveniently "lost" in the contra camps, yet another method by which the lawless band in Washington evades the weak Congressional restrictions on their thuggery.[19] The Libyan provocation too was a success, enabling US forces to sink several Libyan boats, killing more than 50 Libyans, and, it was hoped, to incite Qaddafi to acts of terror against Americans, as was subsequently claimed.

While the US forces were successful in killing many Libyans, they were singularly unable to rescue survivors. The task was apparently not impossible, since 16 survivors from the US attack were rescued from a lifeboat by a Spanish oil tanker.[20]

The official purpose of the US military operation was to establish the right of passage in the Gulf of Sidra, perfect nonsense, since dispatch of a naval flotilla was hardly the necessary or appropriate means to achieve this end; in fact, a declaration would have sufficed. Were further steps deemed necessary for some reason, lawful means were readily available. If someone has a dispute with his or her neighbour over rights to some property, there are two ways to proceed: one is to take the matter to the Courts, the second is to pick up a gun and kill the neighbour. The first option was surely available in the case of the Gulf of Sidra. Since there is plainly no urgency, it was possible to resort to legal means to establish the right of innocent passage. But a violent terrorist state will naturally observe different priorities.

The US position is dubious on narrower grounds. The press continually speaks of "the law of the sea," but Libya shot at US planes, not US ships, and "the law of the air" barely exists. States make various claims in this regard. The US, for example, claims a 200-mile Air Defence Identification Zone within which it has the right to exercise "self-defence" against intruding aircraft judged to be hostile. There is no doubt that US aircraft were well within 200 miles of Libyan territory — 40 miles, the Pentagon claims — and that they were hostile, so that by US standards, Libya was within its rights to intercept them. The point was noted by the conservative legal scholar Alfred Rubin of the Fletcher School at Tufts University, who commented that "by sending in aircraft we went beyond what we were clearly authorized to do under the Law of the Sea" in "an unnecessary provocation."[21] But for a gangster state, such matters are irrelevant, and the exercise was a success, domestically at least.

The extent of the provocation in the Gulf of Sidra was made clear by Pentagon spokesman Robert Sims, who said "that US policy is to shoot at any Libyan boat that enters international waters in the Gulf of Sidra for as long as the US naval exercise in that region continues — no matter how far away the boat might be from US ships." "Given the 'hostile intent' displayed by Libya when it tried to shoot down US warplanes," Sims stated, any Libyan military vessel is "a threat to our forces."[22] In short, the US maintains the right of "self-defence" against any Libyan vessel that approaches its naval armada off the Libyan coast, but Libya does not have a right of self-defence in air space comparable to that claimed by the US.

There is more to the story. David Blundy interviewed British engineers in Tripoli who were repairing the Russian-installed radar system. One, who says he was monitoring the incident throughout on the radar screens (which, contrary to Pentagon claims, were not rendered inoperative), reports that "he saw American warplanes cross not only into the 12 miles of Libyan territorial waters, but over Libyan land as well." "'I watched the planes fly approximately eight miles into Libyan air space,' he said. 'I don't think the Libyans had any choice but to hit back. In my opinion they were reluctant to do so'." The engineer added that "American warplanes made their approach using a normal civil airline traffic route and followed in the wake of a Libyan airliner, so that its radar blip would mask them on the Libyan radar screen."[23]

No hint of this information appeared in the national press, to my knowledge, apart from a typically excellent report by Alexander Cockburn, playing his usual role of personal antidote to media subservience and distortion. Blundy's article was not mysteriously missed by the US press. It was cited by Joseph Lelyveld of the *New York Times*, but with its crucial element entirely omitted.[24]

The Bombing of Libya

One likely consequence of the Gulf of Sidra operation was to elicit acts of Libyan terrorism in retaliation. These would then have the effect of inducing a state of terror in the United States and, with some luck, in Europe as well, setting the stage for the next escalation. The bombing of the La Belle discotheque in West Berlin on 5th April 1986, with one American and one Turk killed, was immediately blamed on Libya, and was then used as a pretext for the 14th April bombing of Tripoli and Benghazi, with about 100 Libyans killed, neatly timed the day before the House vote on contra aid. In case the audience missed the point, Reagan's speech writers made it explicit. Addressing the American Business Conference on 15th April, he said: "And I would remind the House voting this week that this arch-terrorist has sent $400 million and an arsenal of weapons and advisers into Nicaragua to bring his war home to the United States. He has bragged that he is helping the Nicaraguans because they fight America on its own ground."[25] The idea that the "mad dog" is bringing his war home to the US by providing arms to people the US is attacking with its terrorist proxy army was a nice touch, which passed without notable comment, but the PR operation did not, for once, succeed in steamrollering Congress, though the bombing of Libya did enflame chauvinist passions. This consequence was largely attributable, perhaps, to the rampant anti-Arab racism in the United States and the absence of any sane reaction to earlier episodes of manufactured hysteria over Qaddafi's real and alleged crimes.

The 14th April attack was the first bombing in history staged for prime time television. As the subsequently published record shows, the bombing raids were carefully timed so that they would begin precisely at 7pm Eastern Standard Time — as they did; that is, precisely at the moment when all three national television channels broadcast their national news, which was of course pre-empted as agitated anchor men switched to Tripoli for direct eyewitness reports of the exciting events. As soon as the raids ended, the White House had Larry Speakes address a press conference, followed by other dignitaries, ensuring total domination of the propaganda system during the crucial early hours.

One might argue that the Administration took a gamble in this transparent PR operation, since journalists might have asked some difficult questions, but the White House was justly confident that nothing untoward would occur and its faith in the servility of the media proved to be warranted.

Questions could have been raised, surely. To mention only the most obvious one, Speakes stated that the US knew on 4th April that the East Berlin Libyan "People's Bureau" had informed Tripoli that an attack would take place in Berlin the following day, and that it then informed Tripoli that the La Belle discotheque bombing had taken place, as planned. Thus the US knew on 4th-5th April — with certainty, the White House alleged — that Libya was directly responsible for the disco bombing. One might have asked, then, why the reports of US and West German investigations from 5th April to the moment of the attack consistently stated that there were at most suspicions of Libyan involvement. In fact, every journalist listening to the Administration story had in his or her hands — unless we assume the most astonishing incompetence on the part of the news rooms — a report from Berlin which came across the wires at 6.28pm EST, half an hour before the bombing, stating that "the Allied military command (in West Berlin) reported no developments in the investigation of the disco bombing" and that "US and West German officials have said Libya — *possibly* through its embassy in Communist-ruled East Berlin — is *suspected* of involvement in the bombing of the La Belle nightclub" (my emphasis).[26] Some journalists might have asked, then, how it was that just prior to the attack, the US and West Germany still had at most suspicions of Libyan involvement — as throughout the preceding period — while on 4th-5th April, ten days earlier, they had certain knowledge of it. But no embarrassing questions were asked then, nor have they been since, and the relevant facts have been largely suppressed.

Reagan stated on the evening of 14th April that "our evidence is direct, it is precise, it is irrefutable" — just as "We have the evidence, and (Qaddafi) knows it" in the case of the Libyan hit-men, not to speak of the Sandinista involvement in drug-peddling, their announcement of a "revolution without frontiers," the support of Helmut Kohl and Bettino Craxi for the Libyan attack (angrily denied by "shocked" officials in Germany and Italy),[27] and numerous other fabrications of an Administration that has broken the usual records for deceit, but continues "to commit any crime, to lie, to cheat" — in the words of the titular leadership, referring to his Stalinist models — to achieve its ends, confident that the occasional exposure in the small print, well after the fact, will not prevent the constant stream of lies from setting the terms of debate and leaving the appropriate impressions firmly implanted, exactly as it does.

Reactions to the Bombing

Beyond the borders, discipline does not reign. In Germany, a week after Washington had stated its certain knowledge 10 days earlier of Libyan responsibility for the disco bombing, *Der Spiegel* reported that the famed telephone intercepts apparently do not exist and that West Berlin intelligence has only suspicions about Libyan involvement, also suspecting "rival groups of drug dealers" among other possibilities, including neo-Nazi groups. Washington's war is "a means of politics," "insofar as the enemy is as small as Grenada and Libya — and the adversary is as ideal a scoundrel as

Qaddafi," and no European leader should have any illusions that Europe's concerns or interests will be considered if the US decides to escalate international violence, even to the level of a final World War, editor Rudolf Augstein adds.[28] In an interview on 28th April with a reporter from the US Army journal *Stars and Stripes*, Manfred Ganschow, chief of the Berlin *Staatschutz* and head of the 100-man team investigating the disco bombing, stated that "I have no more evidence that Libya was connected with the bombing than I had when you first called me two days after the act. Which is none." He agreed that it was "a highly political case" and hinted at considerable scepticism about what "the politicians" were saying and would say about it.[29] The US press has concealed the doubts expressed by the Berlin investigators, but the careful reader will discern them in the reports of the continuing investigation, as suspects alleged to have Syrian and other connections are investigated.

For much of the world, the US has become an object of considerable fear, as its "bizarre cowboy leader" engages in acts of "madness" in organizing a "band of cutthroats" to attack Nicaragua and playing mad bomber elsewhere, in the words of Canada's leading journal, generally restrained and quite pro-US in tendency.[30] The Reagan Administration is playing on these fears. At the Tokyo Summit of the advanced industrial democracies in May, the Reagan Administration circulated a position paper in which it stated that one reason why Europe would be wise to line up in the US crusade is "the need to do something so that the crazy Americans won't take matters into their own hands again." The threat succeeded in eliciting a statement against terrorism mentioning only Libya by name.[31]

The reaction to the bombing of Libya at home and abroad was sharply different. Expecting the worst, the 12-member European Economic Community called upon the US to avoid "further escalation of military tension in the region with all the inherent dangers." A few hours later, US warplanes struck, as West German Foreign Minister Hans-Dietrich Genscher was on his way to Washington to explain the EEC position. His spokesman stated that "We want to do everything we can to avoid military escalation." The bombing aroused extensive protest throughout most of Europe, including large-scale demonstrations, and evoked editorial condemnation in most of the world. Spain's major journal, the independent *El Pais*, condemned the raid, writing that "The military action of the United States is not only an offence against international law and a grave threat to peace in the Mediterranean, but a mockery of its European allies, who did not find motives for economic sanctions against Libya in a meeting on Monday, despite being previously and without success pressured to adopt sanctions." The conservative *South China Morning Post* in Hong Kong wrote that "President Reagan's cure for the 'mad dog of the Middle East' may prove more lethal than the disease," and his action "may also have lit the fuse to a wider conflagration" in the Middle East. In Mexico City, *El Universal* wrote that the US "has no right to set itself up as the defender of world freedom," urging recourse to legal means through the United Nations. There were many similar reactions.

The US press, in contrast, was overwhelmingly favourable. The *New York Times* wrote that "even the most scrupulous citizens can only approve and applaud the American attacks on Libya," describing this as a just sentence: "the United States has prosecuted (Qaddafi) carefully, proportionately — and justly." The evidence for Libyan responsibility for the disco bombing has been "now laid out clearly to the public"; "Then came the jury, the European governments to which the United States went out of its way to send emissaries to share evidence and urge concerted action against the Libyan leader." It is irrelevant, apparently, that the jury was hardly convinced by the evidence, and issued a "judgment" calling on the executioner to refrain from any action. Most governments also condemned the action, though not all. The government-controlled South Africa Broadcasting Corporation said the attack "underlines the commitment the leader of the Western world has made to taking positive action against terrorism"; the US was justified in attacking Qaddafi, "whose name is virtually synonymous with international terrorism." In Israel, Prime Minister Shimon Peres stated that the US action was clearly justified "in self-defence": "If the Libyan Government issues orders to murder American soldiers in Beirut in cold blood, in the middle of the night, what do you expect the United States to do? Sing Hallelujah? Or take action in her defence?" The idea that the US was acting in "self-defence" against an attack on her forces in Beirut two and a half years earlier is an intriguing innovation, even putting aside the circumstances of that earlier act of "terrorism" against the military forces that much of the population saw as imposing the "New Order" that Israel had sought to establish: the rule of right-wing Christians and selected Muslim elites.[32]

In the US, Senator Mark Hatfield denounced the US bombing raid "on a nearly deserted Senate floor," and in a letter to the *New York Times*. Leaders of several major Christian denominations condemned the bombing, but Jewish leaders generally praised it, among them, Rabbi Alexander Schindler, President of the Union of American Hebrew Congregations, who said "the US government 'properly and vigorously responded' to the 'mindless terrorism'" of Qaddafi. Harvard international affairs professor Joseph Nye said Reagan had to respond "to the smoking gun of that Berlin thing. What else do you do about state-supported terrorism?" — such as US-supported terrorism in Central America, for example, where the "smoking gun" is considerably more in evidence. Eugene Rostow supported the bombing as part of a "more active defence against the process of Soviet expansion," a step that was "inevitable and overdue." The "forcible removal of the Qaddafi regime," he explained, "would be fully justified under the existing rules of international law," since he "has flagrantly and continually violated these rules." "That being the case, every state injured by Libya's actions has the right, alone or with others, to use whatever force is reasonably necessary to put an end to Libya's illegal behaviour. Libya is in the position of the Barbary pirates." He urged NATO to 'issue a declaration on the responsibility of states for illegal acts committed from their territory." *A fortiori*, then, NATO should condemn the Emperor, not just the pirate, and states from Indochina to Central America to the Middle East, among others, should organize to use whatever force is necessary to attack the United States, Israel and other terrorist states.[33]

Real Reasons for the Bombing
The US bombing of Libya has nothing to do with "terrorism", even in the hypocritical Western sense of the word. In fact, it was clear enough that the Gulf of Sidra operation and the bombing of Libyan cities would if anything incite such retail terrorism, one major reason why the likely targets in Europe pleaded with the US to refrain from such action.

This is hardly the first time that violent actions have been executed with the expectation that they would incite retail terrorism. Consider the US-backed Israeli invasion of Lebanon in 1982, undertaken against the background of persistent US-Israeli refusal to permit a peaceful settlement of the Arab-Israeli conflict.[34] After the Israeli-initiated exchange across the Israel-Lebanon border in June 1981 with some 450 Arabs and six Jews killed, the border was "quiet" in the racist terms of American discourse, meaning that there was no PLO response to the many Israeli provocations (including bombing of civilian areas with many killed) undertaken in an effort to elicit a "terrorist act" that could be exploited to justify the planned invasion. Finally, Israel invaded on a pretext in June 1982, proceeding to destroy the civilian base of the PLO in Lebanon and demolish much of what remained of Lebanese society. The goal was to establish a "New Order" under Israeli domination at least in Lebanon and to secure Israel's integration of the occupied territories. It was clear at once that these acts could only have the effect of inspiring what the West calls "terrorism," and indeed, most terrorism, in the Western sense, has since originated in the ruins of Lebanon.

The real reason for the 1982 invasion was not the threat to the northern Galilee, as the sanitized history regularly offered to American audiences pretends, but rather the opposite, as was plausibly explained by Israel's leading specialist on the Palestinians, Yehoshua Porath, shortly after the invasion was launched. The decision to invade, he suggests, "flowed from the fact that the cease-fire had been observed." This was a "veritable catastrophe" for the Israeli government, because it threatened the policy of evading a political settlement. "The government's hope," he continued, "is that the stricken PLO, lacking a logistic and territorial base, will return to its earlier terrorism; it will carry out bombings throughout the world, hijack aircraft, and murder many Israelis," and thus "will lose part of the political legitimacy it has gained" and "undercut the danger" of negotiations with representative Palestinians, which could threaten the policy — shared by both major political groupings — of keeping effective control over the occupied territories.[35] The plausible assumption of the Israeli leadership was that those who shape public opinion in the United States — the only country that counts, now that Israel has chosen to become a mercenary state serving the interests of its provider — could be counted on to obliterate the actual history and portray the terrorist acts resulting from Israeli aggression and atrocities as random acts of violence ascribable to defects in Arab character and culture, if not racial deficiencies. Recent US commentary on terrorism fulfils these natural expectations with some precision.

The basic points are understood well enough in Israel. Prime Minister Yitzhak Shamir stated over Israeli television that Israel went to war because there was "a terrible danger...Not so much a military one as a political one," prompting the fine Israeli satirist B.Michael to write that "the lame excuse of a military danger or a danger to the Galilee is dead," we "have removed the political danger" by striking first, in time; now, "Thank God, there is no one to talk to." Other Israeli commentators have made essentially the same point.

In short, the goals of the war were political, the occupied territories being a prime target. The tale about protecting the border from terrorism is Agitprop, eagerly swallowed by the docile Western media. If Palestinian terrorism can be revived, so much the better. And if we can't pin the blame on Arafat, he can at least be stigmatized as "the founding father of contemporary Palestinian violence,"[36] so that his efforts at a political settlement can be evaded. The attack on Libya may also inspire retail terrorism, which will serve to mobilize domestic and foreign opinion in support of US plans at home and abroad. If Americans react, as they have, by general hysteria, including fear of travelling to Europe where visitors will be at least 100 times as safe as in any American city, this too is a net benefit, for the same reasons.

The real reasons for the US attack on Libya have nothing to do with self-defence against "terrorist attacks" on US forces in Beirut in October 1983, as Shimon Peres would have it, or "self-defence against future attack" in accord with the astonishing doctrine proclaimed by the Reagan Administration to much domestic acclaim. Libya's terrorism is a minor irritant, but Qaddafi has stood in the way of US plans in North Africa, the Middle East and elsewhere: supporting Polisario and anti-US groups in the Sudan, forging a union with Morocco, intervening in Chad,[37] and in general interfering with US efforts to forge a "strategic consensus" in the region, and to impose its will elsewhere. These are real crimes, which must be punished.

More US Violence in Prospect

Furthermore, the Libyan attack had the purpose, and the effect, of preparing opinion at home and abroad for further acts of US violence. The immediate response might be negative, but once absorbed, the level of expectation is heightened and the US can proceed to further escalation.

There are two major areas where such escalation is likely. The first is Central America. While the US proxy army has succeeded in its major task of "forcing (the Sandinistas) to divert scarce resources to the war and away from social programmes," as explained in a rare moment of candour by Administration officials,[38] it is unlikely that it can "cut out the cancer"; hence the threat of successful independent development in terms that might be meaningful to the suffering population of US client states will remain.

Domestic and international pressures prevent the US from attacking directly, as the US attacked South Vietnam in 1962 and later all of Indochina; and the more indirect means of terror, while largely successful in El Salvador, may be inadequate for Nicaragua. It would be natural, then, for the US to move to an arena where it is more likely to prevail: international confrontation. The US has succeeded in cowing most of its allies into refraining from offering any meaningful assistance to Nicaragua, thus largely achieving the intended goal of forcing them to rely on the Soviet bloc for survival. The recent Congressional battle over $100 million of aid was basically a sideshow; a lawless Administration will find ways of funding its terrorist army somehow, whatever Congress legislates. What is important is a more symbolic victory: Congressional authorization for direct CIA involvement and escalation by other means. The obvious means are threats to Soviet and Cuban shipping. Nicaragua would not be able to respond, but the USSR and Cuba might. If they do, the US propaganda system can be counted on to react with outrage over this new proof of Communist aggression, allowing the Administration to construct an international crisis in which, it may be assumed, the USSR will back down, so that Nicaragua will be effectively blockaded. If they do not respond, the same result will be achieved. Of course, the world may go up in smoke, but that is a minor consideration in comparison with the need to excise the cancer. US and European opinion must be prepared for these eventualities. The bombing of Libya turns the ratchet another notch.

The second area where world opinion must be prepared for eventual escalation is the Middle East. The US has blocked political settlement of the Arab-Israeli conflict at least since 1971, when President Sadat of Egypt made his first proposal for a full peace treaty (offering nothing to the Palestinians, and in almost precise accord with US policy as well as the international consensus). In the situation of military confrontation that results from US-Israeli rejectionism, Israel cannot permit any combination of Arab states to approach its military power, since it will face the threat of destruction. The Camp David agreements succeeded in excluding the major Arab state, Egypt, from the conflict, thus allowing Israel to extend its steps towards integrating the occupied territories and to attack its northern neighbour. But Syria remains a growing threat, and sooner or later, Israel will have to act to eliminate it. There is substantial war talk in Israel today, generally alleging Syrian belligerency and threat, but concealing the Israeli intention — indeed, need, as long as a political settlement is averted — to strike to eliminate a possible military rival. The US media follows along, as usual.

Meanwhile, the US government surely wants to leave its options open. It would make sense for an Israeli strike against Syria to be accompanied by US bombing, the former presented as a "pre-emptive strike" in "self-defence against future attack," the latter packaged for Western consumption as "self-defence" against Syrian-inspired terrorism. The purpose of direct US participation would be to warn the Soviet Union that a global war will result from any attempt on their part to support their Syrian ally. European and

US opinion must be prepared for such possible moves. The attack on Libya, and the subsequent propaganda campaigns, help set the stage, leaving the US more free to consider these options if they are later deemed necessary. Again, the likelihood of a nuclear war is not small, but the US has shown repeatedly that it is prepared to face this danger to achieve its ends in the Middle East, as elsewhere.

References

1. "Origins and Fundamental Causes of International Terrorism," UN Secretariat, reprinted in M. Cherif Bassiouni, ed., *International Terrorism and Political Crimes* (Charles Thomas, 1975).
2. William Beecher, *Boston Globe*, April 15, 1986.
3. *Amnesty International Report — 1985* (London, 1985); *Political Killings by Governments* (AI Report, London, 1983); Chris Krueger and Kjell Enge, *Security and Development Conditions in the Guatemalan Highlands* (Washington Office on Latin America, 1985); John Haiman and Anna Meigs, "Qaddafi: Man and Myth," *Africa Events*, Feb. 1986; Alan Nairn, "The Guatemalan Connection," *Progressive*, May 1986. References not given here and below can be found in my *Turning the Tide* (South End, 1985).
4. Edward S. Herman and Frank Brodhead, *Demonstration Elections* (South End, 1984). They define this concept to refer to a device of foreign intervention in which elections are "organized and staged by a foreign power primarily to pacify a restive home population," discussing several other examples as well and showing in detail that they are no less farcical than elections held under Soviet authority. Their term "demonstration elections" was borrowed and radically misused with reference to the election in Nicaragua by Robert Leiken (*New York Review*, Dec. 5, 1985), as part of his campaign in support of the terrorist proxy army established by the US to attack Nicaragua from its Honduran and Costa Rican bases. See Brodhead and Herman's letter, published after half a year's delay along with others by British Parliamentary observers (June 26, 1986), and Leiken's response, tacitly conceding the accuracy of their critique (by evasion) while claiming that they designed their concept "as a way of focusing attention on Western imperialism while diverting it from Soviet imperialism...in line with their apparent belief that there is only one superpower villain"; this is the standard reflex of propagandists whose deceit is exposed, in this case, requiring the suppression of Brodhead and Herman's harsh critique of elections in Poland along with much else. The remainder of Leiken's responses and his articles themselves maintain a comparable level of integrity and merit careful reading for those interested in the workings of the US ideological system.
5. Council on Hemispheric Affairs, *Washington Report on the Hemisphere*, April 16, 1986.
6. See my *Towards a New Cold War* (Pantheon, 1982), for references and discussion, and for more on the topic, Edward S. Herman, *The Real Terror Network* (South End, 1982).
7. I exclude here outright aggression, as in the case of the US attack against South Vietnam, then all of Indochina, the Soviet invasion of Afghanistan, the US-backed invasions of Timor and Lebanon by its Indonesian and Israeli clients, etc.
8. *WP*, June 30, 1985; *Time*, Oct. 11, 1982; Goodman, *NYT*, Feb. 7, 1984. For recent discussion of the astonishing record of Israeli terrorism and the Western response, or lack of it, see my papers "International Terrorism: Image and Reality," delivered at the Frankfurt conference on International Terrorism, April 1986, and "Middle East Terrorism," forthcoming in *Race & Class*.
9. See references of note 6.
10. Editorial, *NYT*, April 20, 1985; *WP*, Jan. 11, 1986; Rabin, *BG*, Jan. 25, 1986; *El Pais* (Madrid), April 25, 1986.
11. *NYT*, June 27; Bob Woodward and Charles R. Babcock, *WP*, May 12; Philip Shenon, *NYT*, May 14, 1985, for CIA denial of involvement "disputed by some Administration and Congressional officials who said that the agency was working with the group at the time of the bombing."

12. Kennedy's programme was limited to the second and third plank of the Reagan agenda; the first, which was enthusiastically supported by Congressional Democrats under Reagan and indeed had already been proposed by Carter, in direct violation of the will of the public, reflects the decline in relative US power in the intervening years. It is no longer feasible to pursue "great societies at home and grand designs abroad," in the words of Kennedy adviser Walter Heller, so the former must be abandoned. On public attitudes, see *Turning the Tide*, chapter 5, and Thomas Ferguson and Joel Rogers, *Atlantic Monthly*, May 1986.

13. *Middle East International*, April 4, 1986.

14. See P. Edward Haley, *Qaddafi and the US Since 1969* (Praeger, 1984), 271f.

15. Larry Speakes, national TV, 7:30PM, April 14; *NYT*, April 16; AP, April 14; *NYT*, April 15; Lewis, *NYT*, April 17; Bernard Weinraub, *NYT*, April 15, 1986.

16. *Op.cit.*, 8, 264.

17. *New Statesman* Aug. 16, 1985.

18. See my *Fateful Triangle* (South End, 1983, 210); Haley, *op.cit.*, who makes a praiseworthy effort to take the comedy seriously.

19. "The Central Intelligence Agency, barred from providing military aid to Nicaragua rebels, secretly funnelled several million dollars to the rebels for political projects over the past year, US government officials say," also allowing "the CIA to maintain a strong influence over the rebel movement, even though a Congressional ban existed from October 1984 through September 1985, prohibiting the agency from spending money 'which would have the effect of supporting, directly or indirectly, military or paramilitary operations in Nicaragua,' the officials said." One purpose of what US officials described as "a major programme" was to "create the aura that [the contras] are an actual political entity among our allies in Europe." Congressman Sam Gejdenson stated that "We suspected that the CIA had never really withdrawn from the scene, but the extent of the agency's direct involvement in the Contra war may astound even the most jaded observer." UNO Documents obtained by AP "show much of UNO's political money going to military organizations allied with the umbrella group" established by the US, while some of the funds were used to pay off Honduran and Costa Rican officials "to enable the rebels to operate in those countries." Much of the money was funnelled through a London-based bank in the Bahamas. AP, April 14; *BG*, April 14, 1986. The disclosures passed without comment. Subsequently, the *Miami Herald* reported that over $2 million of the $27 million provided by Congress for "humanitarian assistance" was used to pay Honduran officers "to turn a blind eye to illegal contra activities on Honduran soil" (editorial, *BG*, May 13, 1986).

20. AP, March 27, citing *El Pais*.

21. Richard Higgins, *BG*, March 25, 1986.

22. Fred Kaplan, *BG*, March 26, 1986.

23. London Sunday Times, April 6, 1986.

24. Cockburn, *Wall St. Journal*, April 17; also *Nation*, April 26, 1986. Lelyveld, *NYT*, April 18, 1986.

25. *NYT*, April 16, 1986.

26. AP, April 14, 1986.

27. James M. Markham, *NYT*, April 25, 1986.

28. *Der Spiegel*, April 21, 1986; the front cover features the phrase "Terror against Terror," a well-known Gestapo slogan, presumably not selected by accident. See also Norman Birnbaum's article, same issue.

29. Text of interview provided by a journalist for *Stars and Stripes* in Germany.

30. *Toronto Globe & Mail*, editorials, March 28, 18, 5, 1986, referring specifically to Nicaragua.

31. See AP, *International Herald Tribune*, May 6, for extensive discussion; *NYT*, May 6, 1986, a briefer mention, and the text of the statement.

32. AP, April 14; survey of world press reaction, AP, April 15; survey of US editorial reaction, April 16; editorial, *NYT*, April 15, 1986; Peres, *NYT*, April 16.

33. AP, April 21; *NYT*, April 20; survey of religious reactions, AP, April 17; also April 19, reporting a news conference of 14 religious and community groups in Seattle condemning

the bombing in contrast to support for it by the Western Washington Rabbinic Board; Nye, *BG*, April 16; Rostow, *NYT*, April 27.

34. On the actual road, very different from the fabrications that dominate US discussion, see *Fateful Triangle*, chap. 3. For a detailed account of Israel's rejectionism under the Labor Party in the crucial 1967-73 period, based on the internal record, see Yossi Beilin, *Mechiro shel Ichud* (Tel Aviv, 1985); as this and other sources demonstrate, the story goes back to the early days of the founding of the state.

35. *Ha'aretz*, June 25, 1982; see *Fateful Triangle*, 200f., for further quotes and similar analyses by other Israeli commentators, and for a review of the events leading up to the invasion.

36. *New Republic*, Jan. 20, 1986.

37. The first Libyan intervention followed the dispatch of French Foreign Legion forces, advisers and aircraft (Haley, *op.cit.,* 98.) but French intervention in Africa is legitimate, indeed laudatory; as *Business Week* exulted, French forces help "keep West Africa safe for French, American, and other foreign oilmen" (Aug. 10, 1981), and perform similar services elsewhere.

38. Julia Preston, *BG*, Feb. 9, 1986.

Nicaragua versus USA at the International Court of Justice

Ken Coates

Ken Coates, editor of
ENDpapers, *is joint
secretary of the European
Nuclear Disarmament
Liaison Committee.*

On 27th June 1986, the International Court of Justice delivered its Judgement against the most potent military power in the world.

The case against the United States of America had been brought by Nicaragua, which had suffered from continuous military and para-military onslaughts over a period of years.

There were 15 judges meeting under the presidency of the distinguished Indian jurist, Nagendra Singh. By 12 votes to 3, they decided "that the United States of America, by training, arming, equipping, financing and supplying the *contra* forces or otherwise encouraging, supporting and aiding, military and paramilitary activities in and against Nicaragua, has acted, against the Republic of Nicaragua, in breach of its obligation under customary international law not to intervene in the affairs of another state". The 3 dissenting judges, Oda, Schwebel, and Jennings came from Japan, the USA, and the United Kingdom respectively. The same 3 reaffirmed their dissent from a number of other crucial findings. By 12 votes to 3, the Court decided that the USA had infringed its obligations not to use force against another State by "certain attacks on Nicaraguan territory in 1983-84, namely attacks on Puerto Sandino on 13th September and 14th October 1983; an attack on Corinto on 10th October 1983; an attack on Potosi Naval Base on 4th/5th January 1984; an attack on San Juan del Sur on 7th March 1984; attacks on patrol boats at Puerto Sandino on 28th and 30th March 1984; and an attack on San Juan del Norte on 9th April 1984". Again, by 12 votes to 3, the Court found that overflights of Nicaraguan territory, and the laying of mines in Nicaraguan territorial waters were actions contrary to customary international law and violations of sovereignty. The mining was also an interruption of "peaceful maritime commerce, and a breach of a 20-year old Treaty between Nicaragua and the USA". This last complaint found the solitary US judge alone in opposition.

Surprisingly,even the American judge condemned the United States for its failure to publish warnings about mining activities. American patriots might note that on this charge, the single dissenting judge was Oda, the Japanese. Oda it was, who further dissented from the finding that the USA "by producing in 1983 a manual entitled *Operaciones Sicologicas en Guerra de Guerrillas*, and disseminating it to *contra* forces has encouraged the commission by them of acts contrary to general principles of humanitarian law". Whilst condemning the manual, the 14 judges felt that they were not entitled to impute to the Americans the responsibility for any actions which might subsequently be based upon its advice.

Again by 12 votes to 3, the Court decided that the United States trade embargo breached the 1956 Treaty of Friendship, Commerce and Navigation. The same more than adequate majority of judges concluded "that the United States of America is under a duty immediately to cease and to refrain from such acts as may constitute breaches of the foregoing legal obligations;" and more: "that the United States of America is under an obligation to make reparation to the Republic of Nicaragua for all injury caused to Nicaragua by the breaches of obligation under customary international law enumerated above". Reparations were also due for injuries in breach of the Treaty of Friendship, Commerce and Navigation.

The International Court is the highest judicial body of the United Nations. It was established at the founding conference in San Francisco in 1945, and its statute formed part of the Charter of the UN. 47 States accept the compulsory jurisdiction of the Court in all legal disputes concerning not only the interpretation of Treaties and questions of international law, but also on the existence of facts which, if established, might breach international obligations. These States are also pledged to accept rulings on the nature of or extent of reparations for breaches of international obligations. Among the 47 are numbered both Nicaragua and the United States. In addition, several members of NATO have registered on this list. They are: Belgium, Canada, Denmark, Luxemburg, Netherlands, Norway, Portugal, and the United Kingdom.

The United States, in initially accepting compulsory jurisdiction, reserved its position in respect of disputes arising under multilateral Treaties, unless all the parties to such Treaties were also parties in the case before the Court, or unless the American Government specifically signified its agreement to jurisdiction. But in 1984, the American Government reversed this decision and refused to recognize the competence of the International Court of Justice in the case brought against it by Nicaragua. The Court, in pressing on with its hearings, restricted its consideration of the dispute to those matters directly pertaining to the two parties before it, excluding claims involving multilateral Treaties, and thus honouring the original conditions under which the US Government had accepted its jurisdiction.

Of course, the Court's decision, from the moment of its announcement, could not avoid provoking reflection on certain very broad multilateral agreements. The most important of these is certainly the United Nations

Charter itself. Chapter 1 of this Charter lays down purposes and principles, which include the commitment that all members "shall settle their international disputes by peaceful means", that all "shall refrain in their international relations from the threat or use of force against the territorial integrity or political independence of any State", and that "all members shall give the United Nations every assistance in any action it takes in accordance with the present Charters ...". Although the International Court was ruling on a specific dispute, and in spite of the fact that it deliberately refrained from pronouncing on its implications for the UN, it is difficult to avoid the conclusion that its findings show that the United States has not been behaving consistently with the Charter. It may be argued that any contravention would be purged if the United States were to accept and implement the Court's decision. But defiance of these decisions marks a qualitative deterioration in the case, and must surely from thence forward place the United States in a position of non-compliance with the Charter. American intervention might conceivably have been thought by some ill-informed persons (bizarre though this view must seem) to have been consonant with the UN Charter before the Court pronounced its judgements. But after that moment, until it came into compliance, there could be no doubt that the US Government was in fundamental conflict with the Court, and thus with the UN Charter itself, under which the Court was established.

It is at this point that other multilateral agreements are affected. Most significant of these is the North Atlantic Treaty, whose members have always claimed that they act strictly in accordance with the principles of the United Nations. The preamble of the North Atlantic Treaty specifically reaffirms "faith in the purposes and principles of the Charter of the United Nations". Article 1 undertakes "as set forth in the Charter of the United Nations to settle any international disputes...by peaceful means in such a manner that international peace and security, and justice, are not endangered, and to refrain...from the threat or use of force in any manner inconsistent with the purpose of the United Nations". It is for this reason that members of the North Atlantic Treaty Organization must be thought to need some explanations from the United States Government. As soon as the Russell Foundation obtained a copy of the judgement of the International Court of Justice, it wrote to the NATO Prime Ministers about this matter. The questions involved were very simple. The first was "Do you believe that the North Atlantic Treaty should be observed by all signatories?" The second was, "If so, what steps do you think might be appropriate to bring the United States of America into compliance with it?" On 21st July 1986, Mrs.Thatcher's Private Secretary replied:

"The Prime Minister has asked me to reply to your letter of 8 July about the finding of the International Court of Justice in the case brought by Nicaragua against the United States.

The Court decided that it had no jurisdiction to rule on whether the US actions complained of by Nicaragua breached the United Nations Charter or other multilateral treaties. As you know, Article 1 of the North Atlantic

Treaty simply reiterates obligations undertaken under the UN Charter.

I enclose a copy of the statement commenting on the ICJ judgement issued by the Foreign and Commonwealth Office on 27 June."

Mr. Powell enclosed an interesting memorandum from a Foreign and Colonial Office spokesman, which indicates that the British Foreign Office found the International Court's reasoning somewhat persuasive:

"FCO Spokesman: Friday 27 June, 2145 BST

ICJ JUDGEMENT: US/NICARAGUA

1. We have only just received the text of the judgement in this case. The Court has obviously considered the case very carefully and has reviewed thoroughly the evidence and facts presented to it.

2. The Court has now delivered a reasoned and detailed judgement. It is lengthy and will require careful study. Our reaction to it will reflect our adherence to the rules of international law which is fundamental to our foreign policy.

3. For many years we have accepted the jurisdiction of the Court and have invariably accepted its judgements in cases to which the UK was a party. We believe it plays a valuable role in international relations.

4. We note that the Court's decision is confined to customary international law and the Treaty of Friendship, Commerce and Navigation between the US and Nicaragua. We note that the Court was always unanimous over its findings with respect to the Treaty and that there was a substantial majority with respect to customary international law."

In the light of the Foreign Office's reaction to the judgement, we did not find the Prime Minister's response totally persuasive, and we wrote again on 23rd July seeking further clarification:

I received a letter from Mr. Powell, in reply to my own enquiry of the 8th July concerning the International Court's findings in the case of Nicaragua versus the United States.

Mr. Powell informs me that the Court decided it had no jurisdiction "to rule on whether the US actions complained of by Nicaragua breached the United Nations Charter or other multilateral treaties". This, however, is not the point. The Court was ruling about past behaviour, and it found that the United States "is under a duty immediately to cease" such behaviour, as well as to pay reparations for previous infractions. The question which affects the North Atlantic Treaty does not concern past behaviour, but future behaviour.

Refusal to accept a decision of the International Court of Justice, the principal judicial organ of the United Nations, is presumably to act in "a manner inconsistent with the purposes of the United Nations".

If the Government intends to follow the guidelines laid down by the Foreign and Colonial Office spokesman on Friday 29th June, which you kindly passed on to me, then it is difficult to see how we can react in 'adherence to the rules of international law' if we make no effort to enforce the terms of the North Atlantic Treaty, which will have been breached by a refusal to act upon the Court's decision.

Before that decision, the United States might or might not have been in breach of the Treaty, and as Mr. Powell rightly says, this matter was not resolved at The Hague. But things are quite different after the judgement, which presumably defines the attitude of the United Nations, since it represents the ultimate legal authority within that body. In short, how can one defy the International Court of Justice and observe Article 1 of the North Atlantic Treaty?"

On 4th August Mr.Powell replied on behalf of the Prime Minister, in the following terms:

"The Prime Minister has asked me to reply to your letter of 23 July about the International Court of Justice findings in the case of Nicaragua versus the United States.

Your views have been noted.

It has been a central plank of British foreign policy since 1949 to support the NATO Alliance. I can reassure you that this support will be fully maintained."

Evidently, Mrs.Thatcher did not wish to discuss the issue further, since she made no effort to answer the questions. But neither did she contradict the arguments which gave rise to them.

Lord Carrington, the Secretary General of NATO, also replied in a somewhat defensive vein. On 25th July he wrote:

"I have given thought to your letter of 8th July in which you suggest that the International Court's recent ruling on certain issues raised by Nicaragua might also raise questions about US compliance with Article I of the NATO Treaty.

It would not be appropriate for me to comment in substance on the legal and political implications of the ruling of the International Court; but it may be worth recalling that the case was one in which the United States denied that the Court had jurisdiction, did not therefore present its side of the case, and maintains that its actions in Central America are fully consistent with UN principles and international law, particularly as regards assistance in cases of collective self-defence.

As far as the North Atlantic Alliance is concerned, I think most people would find the linkage you propose rather artificial given the US's long-established and strong commitment to the NATO Treaty."

We answered on 14th August:

"Thank you very much indeed for your letter of the 25th July concerning the International Court's rulings on Nicaraguan complaints against the United States.

As you know, the International Court is the highest juridical body of the United Nations Organization constituted under Articles 92-96 of the United Nations Charter. Prior to the Nicaraguan complaint, the United States had accepted its compulsory jurisdiction alongside 46 other States. Among these were Belgium, Canada, Denmark, Luxemburg, Netherlands, Norway, Portugal, and the United Kingdom, all of whom share adherence to the North Atlantic Treaty. According to Article 92 of the UN Charter, the statute of the International Court of Justice 'forms an integral part of the present Charter'. It is therefore difficult to see how a State can defy a Court decision, and remain in conformity with Article 1 of the North Atlantic Treaty.

Are you suggesting that it is 'rather artificial' to expect that Treaties be observed? What is in question is not the United States commitment to the North Atlantic Treaty, but its obedience of the United Nations Charter. Of course, in the world of common-sense, many of us have long suspected that regional alliances such as NATO and the Warsaw Treaty do tend to displace loyalty to the United Nations Organization. But statesmen within these alliances have always denied this. Have you reached the point where it can now be confirmed?"

It took some time before Lord Carrington replied, on the 9th September. He, too, did not wish to involve himself in any more discussion:

"Thank you for your further letter about the International Court's recent ruling on Nicaraguan complaints against the United States. I have nothing to add to what I wrote to you in July."

Perhaps he had already said too much, however. If it is the view of the Secretary General of NATO that the United States might be justified in denying jurisdiction to the International Court of Justice, and in refusing to present its side of the case, then isn't the North Atlantic Treaty Organization taking sides against the British Foreign Office, which adjudged matters very differently? The Foreign and Colonial Office may not have finished its "careful study", but its initial reaction of 22nd June sits uneasily with the idea that the International Court Judgement can simply be disregarded. In the beginning, at least, the Foreign and Colonial Office was obviously predisposed to take the Judgement rather seriously.

Some other NATO allies also preferred to reserve their positions. A letter to Chancellor Kohl along the same lines as that to Mrs.Thatcher, produced on 30th July this response from the German Foreign Office:

"The Federal Chancellor has asked the Foreign Office to acknowledge receipt of your letter of 8th July 1986.

The FRG is not a party to the conflict in Central America and did not take part in the proceedings mentioned by you before the International Court of Justice in The Hague. It therefore takes up no position regarding the details of the proceedings and the verdict of the Court.

Besides, the Federal Government has always stressed that it advocates strengthening international organization and international jurisdiction and universality of civil rights. Its policy in Central America is orientated towards the basic aims of peace through dialogue and development through economic co-operation. In this the Federal Government is conscious of being in agreement with its European partners."

As if this might not be clear enough, a further response from Dr.Hellbeck, in the Foreign Office, was sent on the 13th August:

"Thank you for your letter to the Federal Chancellor of 8th July 1986. The Foreign Office has been asked to reply.

The content of the judgement of the International Court of 27th June is of course known to the Foreign Office. It was issued in a case brought by Nicaragua against the USA. The Federal Republic was not a participant in this case. There is therefore no reason for the Federal Government to comment either directly or indirectly on the result."

The problem with this response is not simply that it does not answer the question. Let us make an analogy with any similar action taking place in a a national court, within national jurisdiction. Quite evidently, representatives of government could not possibly pronounce themselves to be indifferent to the enforcement of court decisions, simply because they themselves were not parties in a dispute. Cynics will tell us that the response of the German Government merely highlights the difference between national law and international law. International law, we are often told, is unenforceable.

This may be strictly true, but attitudes to international law none the less reveal a very great deal about the direction and commitment of the authorities involved. It could certainly be argued that European governments need to take up a strongly supportive policy to the International Court of Justice, and to the wider question of the enforcement of international agreements and obligations. The countries in the European zone, which are seeking closer economic integration and association, cannot afford to be negligent on this matter. To profess oneself indifferent to the enforceability of an International Court decision, when it affects the conduct of one's close ally, is not very consistent with this need. European statesmen are likely, if they follow this trend, to find that they have greater and greater dependence on an enforceable framework of international law governing economic decisions, at the same time that their political alliances render international legalities more and more inconvenient.

Other Governments were more aware of this problem. On 20th August, Mr.A.J.Ettema, of the Dutch Ministry of Foreign Affairs, offered a very different kind of response:

"In response to your letter of 8 July 1986 I wish to point out the following:

The Netherlands attaches great importance to the principle of peaceful settlement of disputes and recognizes the important role of the International Court of Justice in this field. Accordingly it has, on a reciprocal basis accepted the compulsory jurisdiction of the ICJ and hopes that those states which have so far not done so, will also decide to recognize the Court's compulsory jurisdiction in the future. In the Netherlands' view rulings of the Court in cases which fall under its compulsory jurisdiction and in other cases which have been laid before the ICJ should be honoured by the parties involved.

With regard to the conclusion you draw from the Court's ruling, i.e. that the United States would be in breach of Article 1 of the North Atlantic Treaty as this Article refers to the United Nations Charter, I would like to underline that the Court explicitly decided (by eleven votes to four) that it had no jurisdiction to adjudicate the dispute on the basis of the United Nations Charter."

This letter arrived in England while I was abroad so that I could not reply until 9th September. Although the attitude of the Dutch Government showed altogether greater concern for the International Court of Justice, I found it necessary to repeat a point I had tried to explain in the earlier correspondence with Lord Carrington and Mrs.Thatcher.

"Thank you for your kindness in replying to my letter of 8th July, concerning the International Court of Justice findings in the case of Nicaragua versus the United States. Of course I welcome the position of the Netherlands Government on this judgement, and believe that this is an entirely proper response to the issues involved.

However, I think that I did not make clear the gravamen of my point about the United States breaching Article 1 of the North Atlantic Treaty. Of course, you are right about the position of the Court concerning its lack of jurisdiction to adjudicate the dispute on the basis of the United Nations Charter. Whatever we think about that decision it is now a given fact. But this had nothing to do with my complaint: which does not concern what happened before the Court reached its decision, but what has been happening since that time. If the United States' Government had accepted the Court's findings, or even if it had agreed to comply with them, whilst continuing to dispute them in argument, then it might be argued that the United States remained in compliance with Article 1 of the North Atlantic Treaty. But the defiance of the International Court must surely constitute a breach of Article 1, since the International Court is the highest juridical body of the United Nations? In other words, the problem is not one over which the International Court needs to make any pronouncement: either the United Nations institutions are enforced, or they are not, and failure to enforce them contravenes the spirit of the Treaty.

Do you think this reasoning is fallacious?

I should greatly value your advice on this matter."

Two other Prime Ministers gave strong support to the International Court of Justice, and to its Nicaraguan judgement. From Norway, Eldrid Nordbo replied on behalf of the Prime Minister on 9th September:

"The Prime Minister has asked me to thank you for your letter of 8 July 1986 about the judgement of the International Court of Justice concerning military and paramilitary activities in and against Nicaragua.

The Court has delivered a judgement based on sources of international law which it shall apply in accordance with its statutes. The Norwegian Government is firmly supporting the Court and believes that its role should be strengthened. At present the Government does not see any need for adopting a position on sources of international law, non-applicable or applicable, which are extraneous to the completed deliberations of the Court."

From Spain, Mr.J.Julio Feo replied on behalf of Felipe Gonzalez on 9th September:

"I'm pleased to acknowledge receipt of your kind letter of 8 July to the Prime Minister, and at the same time to express his appreciation of the task that the Foundation has been developing in favour of international peace and justice.

The Spanish Government's position regarding the Central American conflict is well-known and has been repeatedly demonstrated in every appropriate international forum, and lately in the debate which took place at Nicaragua's initiative in the Security Council. Our stance arises from the premise that international law and the principles contained in the United Nations Charter must be fully respected by every State. The need to respect them is particularly evident in conflicts which place in danger international peace and security. In these circumstances our best guarantee to find solutions is to abide by international law and to observe the principles of the Charter, according to the guidelines provided by the competent bodies of the United Nations.

The Spanish Government is firmly convinced that it is necessary to reach a full, regional, peaceful, and negotiated solution in Central America. In this spirit we continue to actively support the task that the Contadora group has been developing for more than three years, and that, after the establishment of the Support Group, has come to represent the feelings of every Latin American democracy, and has produced a strong response from the international community. The Spanish Government has been working within this same line, and will go on working, both in its contacts with those Governments directly involved and with the European Political Co-operation."

At the moment of writing, this international correspondence ceases here.

But we imagine that there will be further replies, and we hope that other people will join us in pressing for answers. Of course, there are very many people who believe that States are completely cynical when they conclude Treaties, and that it is a matter of rather small consequence that such Treaties are violated. We are bound to accept that such violations happen, and that international law is not easily, and certainly not neutrally, enforceable. But this is not a situation which we should uncomplainingly accept. The project for a United Nations Organization, properly understood, committed its protagonists to a long struggle for acceptable standards of international behaviour. In democratic countries, this struggle benefits from the active involvement of concerned citizens. It seems to us that people living in countries which have endorsed the North Atlantic Treaty should be encouraged to insist upon the enforcement of its firm commitment to the United Nations. Failure to pursue this question, surely, means compliance in illegality and growing international brigandage.

Certainly since the United States Government decided that it would not respond to Nicaragua's complaints to the International Court, we have seen a fierce escalation of violence in other areas. In Libya, to take only the most evident example, direct American action followed the unilateral Libyan declaration of territorial control over the Gulf of Sidra/Sirte. Neither this decision, nor even the more difficult question of allegations concerning international terrorism were matters beyond the reach of the International Court of Justice. Why did the Americans not seek recourse to this Court? Of course the main answer is very plain: repudiation of the Court's competence in one area is extremely difficult to square with assertion of that competence in another. Already the United States was in some difficulty, because it had enthusiastically (and understandably) welcomed the earlier International Court judgement in its own dispute with Iran, a few years earlier. Having now denied the relevance of international law to cover one problem, there followed an inexorable retreat to policies of force. These, of course, raise wider issues. In a world bristling with nuclear weapons, these are frightening to contemplate.

Military and Paramilitary Activities in and against Nicaragua

Judgment of the International Court of Justice

On 27th June 1986 the International Court delivered its judgment in the case of Nicaragua versus the United States of America. The United States Government refused to recognise the proceedings, and presented no evidence. By convincing majorities, however, the judges reached the following conclusions.

Operative part of the Court's Judgment

The Court

(1) By eleven votes to four,

decides that in adjudicating the dispute brought before it by the Application filed by the Republic of Nicaragua on 9th April 1984, the Court is required to apply the "multilateral treaty reservation" contained in proviso (c) in the declaration of acceptance of jurisdiction made under Article 36, paragraph 2, of the Statute of the Court by the United States of America deposited on 26th August 1946;

In favour: President Nagendra Singh; Vice-President de Lacharriere; Judges Lachs, Oda, Ago, Schwebel, Sir Robert Jennings, Mbaye, Bedjaoui and Evensen; Judge ad hoc Colliard;

Against: Judges Ruda, Elias, Sette-Camara and Ni.

(2) By twelve votes to three,

rejects the justification of collective self-defence maintained by the United States of America in connection with the military and paramilitary activities in and against Nicaragua the subject of this case;

In favour: President Nagendra Singh; Vice-President de Lacharriere; Judges Lachs, Ruda, Elias, Ago, Sette-Camara, Mbaye, Bedjaoui, Ni and Evensen; Judge ad hoc Colliard;

Against: Judges Oda, Schwebel and Sir Robert Jennings.

(3) By twelve votes to three,

decides that the United States of America, by training, arming, equipping, financing and supplying the *contra* forces or otherwise encouraging, supporting and aiding military and paramilitary activities in and against Nicaragua, has acted, against the Republic of Nicaragua, in breach of its obligation under customary international law not to intervene in the affairs of another State;

In favour: President Nagendra Singh; Vice-President de Lacharriere; Judges Lachs, Ruda, Elias, Ago, Sette-Camara, Mbaye, Bedjaoui, Ni and Evensen; Judge ad hoc Colliard;

Against: Judges Oda, Schwebel and Sir Robert Jennings.

(4) By twelve votes to three,

decides that the United States of America, by certain attacks on Nicaraguan territory in 1983-84, namely attacks on Puerto Sandino on 13th September and 14th October 1983; an attack on Corinto on 10th October 1983; an attack on Potosi Naval Base on 4th/5th January 1984; an attack on San Juan del Sur on 7th March 1984; attacks on patrol boats at Puerto Sandino on 28th and 30th March 1984; and an attack on San Juan del Norte on 9th April 1984; and further by those acts of intervention referred to in subparagraph (3) hereof which involve the use of force, has acted, against the Republic of Nicaragua, in breach of its obligation under customary international law not to use force against another State.

In favour: President Nagendra Singh; Vice-President de Lacharriere; Judges Lachs, Ruda, Elias, Ago, Sette-Camara, Mbaye, Bedjaoui, Ni and Evensen; Judge ad hoc Colliard;

Against: Judges Oda, Schwebel and Sir Robert Jennings.

(5) By twelve votes to three,

decides that the United States of America, by directing or authorizing overflights of Nicaraguan territory, and by the acts imputable to the United States referred to in subparagraph (4) hereof, has acted, against the Republic of Nicaragua, in breach of its obligation under customary international law not to violate the sovereignty of another State;

In favour: President Nagendra Singh; Vice-President de Lacharriere; Judges Lachs, Ruda, Elias, Ago, Sette-Camara, Mbaye, Bedjaoui, Ni and Evensen; Judge ad hoc Colliard;

Against: Judges Oda, Schwebel and Sir Robert Jennings

(6) By twelve votes to three,

decides that, by laying mines in the internal or territorial waters of the Republic of Nicaragua during the first months of 1984, the United States of America has acted, against the Republic of Nicaragua, in breach of its obligations under customary international law not to use force against another State, not to intervene in its affairs, not to violate its sovereignty and not to interrupt peaceful maritime commerce;

In favour: President Nagendra Singh; Vice-President de Lacharriere; Judges Lachs, Ruda, Elias, Ago, Sette-Camara, Mbaye, Bedjaoui, Ni and Evensen; Judge ad hoc Colliard;

Against: Judges Oda, Schwebel and Sir Robert Jennings.

(7) By fourteen votes to one,

decides that, by the acts referred to in subparagraph (6) hereof, the United States of America has acted, against the Republic of Nicaragua, in breach of its obligations under Article XIX of the Treaty of Friendship, Commerce and Navigation between the United States of America and the Republic of Nicaragua signed at Managua on 21st January 1956;

In favour: President Nagendra Singh; Vice-President de Lacharriere; Judges Lachs, Ruda, Elias, Oda, Ago, Sette-Camara, Sir Robert Jennings, Mbaye, Bedjaoui, Ni and Evensen; Judge ad hoc Colliard;

Against: Judge Schwebel.

(8) By fourteen votes to one,

decides that the United States of America, by failing to make known the existence and location of the mines laid by it, referred to in subparagraph (6) hereof, has acted in breach of its obligations under customary international law in this respect;

In favour: President Nagendra Singh; Vice-President de Lacharriere; Judges Lachs, Ruda, Elias, Ago, Sette-Camara, Schwebel, Sir Robert Jennings, Mbaye, Bedjaoui, Ni and Evensen; Judge ad hoc Colliard;

Against: Judge Oda.

(9) By fourteen votes to one,

finds that the United States of America, by producing in 1983 a manual entitled "Operaciones sicologicas en guerra de guerrillas", and disseminating it to *contra* forces, has encouraged the commission by them of acts contrary to general principles of humanitarian law; but does not find a basis for concluding that any such acts which may have been committed are imputable to the United States of America as acts of the United States of America;

In favour: President Nagendra Singh; Vice-President de Lacharriere; Judges Lachs, Ruda, Elias, Ago, Sette-Camara, Schwebel, Sir Robert Jennings, Mbaye, Bedjaoui, Ni and Evensen; Judge ad hoc Colliard.

Against: Judge Oda.

(10) By twelve votes to three,

decides that the United States of America, by the attacks on Nicaraguan territory referred to in subparagraph (4) hereof, and by declaring a general embargo on trade with Nicaragua on 1st May 1985, has committed acts calculated to deprive of its object and purpose the Treaty of Friendship, Commerce and Navigation between the Parties signed at Managua on 21st January 1956;

In favour: President Nagendra Singh; Vice-President de Lacharriere; Judges Lachs, Ruda, Elias, Ago, Sette-Camara, Mbaye, Bedjaoui, Ni and Evensen; Judge ad hoc Colliard;

Against: Judges Oda, Schwebel and Sir Robert Jennings.

(11) By twelve votes to three,

decides that the United States of America, by the attacks on Nicaraguan territory referred to in subparagraph (4) hereof, and by declaring a general embargo on trade with Nicaragua on 1 May 1985, has acted in breach of its obligations under Article XIX of the Treaty of Friendship, Commerce and Navigation between the Parties signed at Managua on 21st January 1956;

In favour: President Nagendra Singh; Vice-President de Lacharriere; Judges Lachs, Ruda, Elias, Ago, Sette-Camara, Mbaye, Bedjaoui, Ni and Evensen; Judge ad hoc Colliard;

Against: Judges Oda, Schwebel and Sir Robert Jennings.

(12) By twelve votes to three,

decides that the United States of America is under a duty immediately to cease and to refrain from all such acts as may constitute breaches of the foregoing legal obligations;

In favour: President Nagendra Singh; Vice-President de Lacharriere;

Judges Lachs, Ruda, Elias, Ago, Sette-Camara, Mbaye, Bedjaoui, Ni and Evensen; Judge ad hoc Colliard;

Against: Judges Oda, Schwebel and Sir Robert Jennings.

(13) By twelve votes to three,

decides that the United States of America is under an obligation to make reparation to the Republic of Nicaragua for all injury to Nicaragua caused by the breaches of obligations under customary international law enumerated above;

In favour: President Nagendra Singh; Vice-President de Lacharriere; Judges Lachs, Ruda, Elias, Ago, Sette-Camara, Mbaye, Bedjaoui, Ni and Evensen; Judge ad hoc Colliard;

Against: Judges Oda, Schwebel and Sir Robert Jennings.

(14) By fourteen votes to one,

decides that the United States of America is under an obligation to make reparation to the Republic of Nicaragua for all the injury caused to Nicaragua by the breaches of the Treaty of Friendship, Commerce and Navigation between the Parties signed at Managua on 21st January 1956;

In favour: President Nagendra Singh; Vice-President de Lacharriere; Judges Lachs, Ruda, Elias, Oda, Ago, Sette-Camara, Sir Robert Jennings, Mbaye, Bedjaoui, Ni and Evensen; Judge ad hoc Colliard;

Against: Judge Schwebel.

(15) By fourteen votes to one,

decides that the form and amount of such reparation, failing agreement between the Parties, will be settled by the Court, and reserves for this purpose the subsequent procedure in the case;

In favour: President Nagendra Singh, Vice-President de Lacharriere; Judges Lachs, Ruda, Elias, Oda, Ago, Sette-Camara, Sir Robert Jennings, Mbaye, Bedjaoui, Ni and Evensen; Judge ad hoc Colliard;

Against: Judge Schwebel.

(16) Unanimously, *recalls* to both Parties their obligation to seek a solution to their disputes by peaceful means in accordance with international law.

SUMMARY OF THE JUDGMENT

I. Qualités (paras. 1 to 17)

II. Background to the dispute (paras. 18-25)

III. The non-appearance of the Respondent and Article 53 of the Statute (paras. 26-31)

The Court recalls that subsequent to the delivery of its Judgment of 26th November 1984 on the jurisdiction of the Court and the admissibility of Nicaragua's Application, the United States decided not to take part in the present phase of the proceedings. This, however, does not prevent the Court from giving a decision in the case, but it has to do so while respecting the requirements of Article 53 of the Statute, which provides for the situation when one of the parties does not appear. The Court's jurisdiction being established, it has in accordance with Article 53 to satisfy itself that the claim of the party appearing is well founded in fact and law. In this respect the

Court recalls certain guiding principles brought out in a number of previous cases, one of which excludes any possibility of a judgment automatically in favour of the party appearing. It also observes that it is valuable for the Court to know the views of the non-appearing party, even if those views are expressed in ways not provided for in the Rules of Court. The principle of the equality of the parties has to remain the basic principle, and the Court has to ensure that the party which declines to appear should not be permitted to profit from its absence.

IV. Justiciability of the dispute (paras. 32-35)

The court considers it appropriate to deal with a preliminary question. It has been suggested that the questions of the use of force and collective self-defence raised in the case fall outside the limits of the kind of questions the Court can deal with, in other words that they are not justiciable. However, in the first place the Parties have not argued that the present dispute is not a "legal dispute" within the meaning of Article 36, paragraph 2, of the Statute, and secondly, the Court considers that the case does not necessarily involve it in the evaluation of political or military matters, which would be to overstep proper judicial bounds. Consequently, it is equipped to determine these problems.

V. The significance of the multilateral treaty reservation (paras. 36-56)

The United States declaration of acceptance of the compulsory jurisdiction of the Court under Article 36, paragraph 2, of the Statute contained a reservation excluding from the operation of the declaration

"disputes arising under a multilateral treaty, unless (1) all parties to the treaty affected by the decision are also parties to the case before the Court, or (2) the United States of America specially agrees to jurisdiction".

In its judgment of 26th November 1984 the Court found, on the basis of Article 79, paragraph 7, of the Rules of Court, that the objection to jurisdiction based on the reservation raised "a question concerning matters of substance relating to the merits of the case" and that the objection did "not possess, in the circumstances of the case, an exclusively preliminary character". Since it contained both preliminary aspects and other aspects relating to the merits, it had to be dealt with at the stage of the merits.

In order to establish whether its jurisdiction was limited by the effect of the reservation in question, the Court hs to ascertain whether any third parties, parties to the four multilateral treaties invoked by Nicaragua, and not parties to the proceedings, would be "affected" by the Judgment. Of these treaties, the Court considers it sufficient to examine the position under the United Nations Charter and the Charter of the Organization of American States.

The Court examines the impact of the multilateral treaty reservation on Nicaragua's claim that the United States has used force in breach of the two Charters. The Court examines in particular the case of El Salvador, for whose benefit primarily the United States claims to be exercising the right of collective self-defence which it regards as a justification of its own conduct towards Nicaragua, that right being endorsed by the United Nations Charter (Art.51) and the OAS Charter (Art.21). The dispute is to this extent a dispute "arising under" multilateral treaties to which the United States, Nicaragua and El Salvador are Parties. It appears clear to the Court that El Salvador would be "affected" by the Court's decision on the lawfulness of the resort by the United States to collective self-defence.

As to Nicaragua's claim that the United States has intervened in its affairs contrary to the OAS Charter (Art.18) the Court observes that it is impossible to say that a ruling on the alleged breach of the Charter by the United States would not "affect" El Salvador.

Having thus found that El Salvador would be "affected" by the decision the Court would have to take on the claims of Nicaragua based on the violations of the two Charters by the United States, the Court concludes that the jurisdiction conferred on it by the United States declaration does not permit it to entertain these claims. It makes it clear that the effect of the reservation is confined to barring the applicability of these two multilateral treaties as multilateral treaty law, and has no further impact on the sources of international law which Article 38 of the Statute requires the Court to apply, including customary international law.

VI. Establishment of the facts: evidence and methods employed by the Court (paras. 57-74)

The Court has had to determine the facts relevant to the dispute. The difficulty of its task derived from the marked disagreement between the Parties, the non-appearance of the Respondent, the secrecy surrounding certain conduct, and the fact that the conflict is continuing. On this last point, the Court takes the view, in accordance with the general principles as to the judicial process, that the facts to be taken into account should be those occurring up to the close of the oral proceedings on the merits of the case (end of September 1985).

With regard to the production of evidence, the Court indicates how the requirements of its Statute — in particular Article 53 — and the Rules of Court have to be met in the case, on the basis that the Court has freedom in estimating the value of the various elements of evidence. It has not seen fit to order an enquiry under Article 50 of the Statute. With regard to certain *documentary material* (press articles and various books), the Court has treated these with caution. It regards them not as evidence capable of proving facts, but as material which can nevertheless contribute to corroborating the existence of a fact and be taken into account to show whether certain facts are matters of public knowledge. With regard to *evidence of witnesses* presented by Nicaragua — five witnesses gave oral evidence and another a written affidavit — one consequence of the absence of the Respondent was that the evidence of the witnesses was not tested by cross-examination. The Court has not treated as evidence any part of the testimony which was a mere expression of opinion as to the probability or otherwise of the existence of a fact not directly known to the witness. With regard in particular to *affidavits* and sworn *statements* made by members of a

Government, the Court considers that it can certainly retain such parts of this evidence as may be regarded as contrary to the interests or contentions of the State to which the witness has allegiance; for the rest such evidence has to be treated with great reserve.

The Court is also aware of the publiction of the United States State Department entitled "Revolution Beyond Our Borders, Sandinista Intervention in Central America" which was not submitted to the Court in any form or manner contemplated by the Statute and Rules of Court. The Court considers that, in view of the special circumstances of this case, it may, within limits, make use of the information in that publication.

VII. The facts imputable to the United States (paras. 75 to 125)

1. The Court examines the allegations of Nicaragua that the *mining of Nicaraguan ports or waters* was carried out by United States military personnel or persons of the nationality of Latin American countries in the pay of the United States. After examining the facts, the Court finds it established that, on a date in late 1983 or early 1984, the President of the United States authorized a United States government agency to lay mines in Nicaraguan ports; that in early 1984 mines were laid in or close to the ports of El Bluff, Corinto and Puerto Sandino, either in Nicaraguan internal waters or in its territorial sea or both, by persons in the pay or acting on the instructions of that agency, under the supervision and with the logistic support of United States agents; that neither before the laying of mines, nor subsequently, did the United States Government issue any public and official warning to international shipping of the existence and location of the mines; and that personal and material injury was caused by the explosion of the mines, which also created a risk causing a rise in marine insurance rates.

2. Nicaragua attributes to the direct action of United States personnel, or persons in its pay, operations against *oil installations, a naval base, etc.*, listed in paragraph 81 of the Judgment. The Court finds all these incidents except three, to be established. Although it is not proved that any United States military personnel took a direct part in the operations, United States agents participated in the planning, direction and support. The imputability to the United States of these attacks appears therefore to the Court to be established.

3. Nicaragua complains of *infringement of its air space* by United States military aircraft. After indicating the evidence available, the Court finds that the only violations of Nicaraguan air space imputable to the United States on the basis of the evidence are high altitude reconnaissance flights and low altitude flights on 7th to 11th November 1984 causing "sonic booms".

With regard to joint military manoeuvres with Honduras carried out by the United States on Honduran territory near the Honduras/Nicaragua frontier, the Court considers that they may be treated as public knowledge and thus sufficiently established.

4. The court then examines the genesis, development and *activities of the contra force*, and the *role of the United States* in relation to it. According to

Nicaragua, the United States "conceived, created and organized a mercenary army, the *contra* force". On the basis of the available information, the Court is not able to satisfy itself that the Respondent State "created" the contra force in Nicaragua, but holds it established that it largely financed, trained, equipped, armed and organized the FDN, one element of the force.

It is claimed by Nicaragua that the United States Government devised the strategy and directed the tactics of the *contra* force, and provided direct combat support for its military operations. In the light of the evidence and the material available to it, the Court is not satisfied that all the operations launched by the *contra* force, at every stage of the conflict, reflected strategy and tactics solely devised by the United States. It therefore cannot uphold the contention of Nicaragua on this point. The Court however finds it clear that a number of operations were decided and planned, if not actually by United States advisers, then at least in close collaboration with them, and on the basis of the intelligence and logistic support which the United States was able to offer. It also established in the Court's view that the support of the United States for the activities of the *contras* took various forms over the years, such as logistic support, the supply of information on the location and movements of the Sandinista troops, the use of sophisticated methods of communication, etc. The evidence does not however warrant a finding that the United States gave direct combat support, if that is taken to mean direct intervention by United States combat forces.

The Court has to determine whether the relationship of the *contras* to the United States Government was such that it would be right to equate the *contras*, for legal purposes, with an organ of the United States Government, or as acting on behalf of that Government. The Court considers that the evidence available to it is insufficient to demonstrate the total dependence of the *contras* on United States aid. A partial dependency, the exact extent of which the Court cannot establish, may be inferred from the fact that the leaders were selected by the United States, and from other factors such as the organization, training and equipping of the force, planning of operations, the choosing of targets and operational support provided. There is no clear evidence that the United States actually exercised such a degree of control as to justify treating the *contras* as acting on its behalf.

5. Having reached the above conclusion, the Court takes the view that the *contras* remain responsible for their acts, in particular the alleged violations by them of *humanitarian law*. For the United States to be legally responsible, it would have to be proved that that State had effective control of the operations in the course of which the alleged violations were committed

6. Nicaragua has complained of certain *measures of an economic nature* taken against it by the Government of the United States, which it regards as an indirect form of intervention in its internal affairs. Economic aid was suspended in January 1981; and terminated in April 1981, the United States acted to oppose or block loans to Nicaragua by international financial bodies; the sugar import quota from Nicaragua was reduced by 90 per cent in

September 1983; and a total trade embargo on Nicaragua was declared by an executive order of the President of the United States on 1st May 1985.

VIII. The conduct of Nicaragua (paras. 126-171)

The Court has to ascertain, as far as possible, whether the activities of the United States complained of, claimed to have been the exercise of collective self-defence, may be justified by certain facts attributable to Nicaragua.

1. The United States has contended that Nicaragua was *actively supporting armed groups operating in certain of the neighbouring countries*, particularly in El Salvador, and specifically in the form of the *supply of arms*, an accusation which Nicaragua has repudiated. The Court first examines the activity of Nicaragua with regard to El Salvador.

Having examined various evidence, and taking account of a number of concordant indications, many of which were provided by Nicaragua itself, from which the Court can reasonably infer the provision of a certain amount of aid from Nicaraguan territory, the Court concludes that support for the armed opposition in El Salvador from Nicaraguan territory was a fact up to the early months of 1981. Subsequently, evidence of military aid from or through Nicaragua remains very weak, despite the deployment by the United States in the region of extensive technical monitoring resources. The Court cannot however conclude that no transport of or traffic in arms existed. It merely takes note that the allegations of arms traffic are not solidly established, and has not been able to satisfy itself that any continuing flow on a significant scale took place after the early months of 1981.

Even though it was established that military aid was reaching the armed opposition in El Salvador from the territory of Nicaragua, it still remains to be proved that such aid is imputable to the authorities of Nicaragua, which has not sought to conceal the possibility of weapons crossing its territory, but denies that this is the result of any deliberate official policy on its part. Having regard to the circumstances characterizing this part of Central America, the court considers that it is scarcely possible for Nicaragua's responsibility for arms traffic on its territory to be automatically assumed. The Court considers it more consistent with the probabilities to recognize that an activity of that nature, if on a limited scale, may very well be pursued unknown to the territorial government. In any event the evidence is insufficient to satisfy the Court that the Government of Nicaragua was responsible for any flow of arms at either period.

2. The United States has also accused Nicaragua of being responsible for *cross-border military attacks* on Honduras and Costa Rica. While not as fully informed on the question as it would wish to be, the Court considers as established that certain trans-border military incursions are imputable to the Government of Nicaragua.

3. The Judgment recalls certain events which happened at the time of the fall of President Somoza, since reliance has been placed on them by the United States to contend that the present Government of Nicaragua is in violation of certain alleged *assurances* given by its immediate predecessor. The Judgment refers in particular to the "Plan to secure peace" sent on 12th

July 1979 by the "Junta of the Government of National Reconstruction" of Nicaragua to the Secretary-General of the OAS, mentioning, *inter alia* , its "firm intention to establish full observance of human rights in our country" and "to call the first free elections our country has known in this century". The United States considers that it has a special responsibility regarding the implementation of these commitments.

IX. The applicable law: customary international law (paras. 172-182)

The Court has reached the conclusion (section V, *in fine*) that it has to apply the multilateral treaty reservation in the United States declaration, the consequential exclusion of multilateral treaties being without prejudice either to other treaties or other sources of law enumerated in Article 38 of the Statute. In order to determine the law actually to be applied to the dispute, it has to ascertain the consequences of the exclusion of the applicability of the multilateral treaties for the definition of the content of the customary international law which remains applicable.

The Court, which has already commented briefly on this subject in the jurisdiction phase (*ICJ Reports 1984*, pp.424 and 425, para.73), develops its initial remarks. It does not consider that it can be claimed, as the United States does, that all the customary rules which may be invoked have a content exactly identical to that of the rules contained in the treaties which cannot be applied by virtue of the United States reservation. Even if a treaty norm and a customary norm relevant to the present dispute were to have exactly the same content, this would not be a reason for the Court to take the view that the operation of the treaty process must necessarily deprive the customary norm of its separate applicability. Consequently, the Court is in no way bound to uphold customary rules only in so far as they differ from the treaty rules which it is prevented by the United States reservation from applying.

In response to an argument of the United States, the Court considers that the divergence between the content of the customary norms and that of the treaty law norms is not such that a judgment confined to the field of customary international law would not be susceptible of compliance or execution by the parties.

X. The content of the applicable law (paras. 183 to 225)

1. Introduction: general observations (paras. 183-186)

The Court has next to consider what are the rules of customary law applicable to the preent dispute. For this purpose it has to consider whether a customary rule exists in the *opinio juris* of States, and satisfy itself that it is confirmed by practice.

2. The prohibition of the use of force, and the right of self-defence (paras. 187 to 201)

The Court finds that both parties take the view that the principles as to the use of force incorporated in the United Nations Charter correspond, in essentials, to those found in customary international law. They therefore accept a treaty-law obligation to refrain in their international relations from the threat or use of force against the territorial integrity or political independence of any State, or in any other manner inconsistent with the purposes of the United Nations (Art.2, para.4, of the Charter). The Court has however to be satisfied that there exists in customary law an *opinio juris* as to the binding character of such abstention. It considers that this *opinio juris* may be deduced from, *inter alia*, the attitude of the Parties and of States towards certain General Assembly resolutions, and particularly resolution 2625 (XXV) entitled "Declarations on Principles of International Law concerning Friendly Relations and Co-operation among States in Accordance with the Charter of the United Nations". Consent to such resolutions is one of the forms of expression of an *opinio juris* with regard to the principle of non-use of force, regarded as a principle of customary international law, independently of the provisions, especially those of an institutional kind, to which it is subject on the treaty-law plane of the Charter.

The general rule prohibiting force established in customary law allows for certain exceptions. The exception of the right of individual or collective self-defence is also, in the view of States, established in customary law, as is apparent for example from the terms of Article 51 of the United Nations Charter, which refers to an "inherent right", and from the declaration in resolution 2625 (XXV). The Parties, who consider the existence of this right to be established as a matter of customary international law, agree in holding that whether the response to an attack is lawful depends on the observance of the criteria of the necessity and the proportionality of the measures taken in self-defence.

Whether self-defence be individual or collective, it can only be exercised in response to an "armed attack". In the view of the Court, that is to be understood as meaning not merely action by regular armed forces across an international border, but also the sending by a State of armed bands on to the territory of another State, if such an operation, because of its scale and effects, would have been classified as an armed attack had it been carried out by regular armed forces. The Court quotes the definition of aggression annexed to General Assembly resolution 3314 (XXIX) as expressing customary law in this respect.

The Court does not believe that the concept of "armed attack" includes assistance to rebels in the form of the provision of weapons or logistical or other support. Furthermore, the Court finds that in customary international law, whether of a general kind or that particular to the inter-American legal system, there is no rule permitting the exercise of collective self-defence in the absence of a request by the State which is a victim of the alleged attack, this being additional to the requirement that the State in question should have declared itself to have been attacked.

3. *The principle of non-intervention (paras. 202 to 209)*

The principle of non-intervention involves the right of every sovereign State to conduct its affairs without outside interference. Expressions of an *opinio juris* of States regarding the existence of this principle are numerous. The Court notes that this principle, stated in its own jurisprudence, has been reflected in numerous declarations and resolutions adopted by international organizations and conferences in which the United States and Nicaragua have participated. The text thereof testifies to the acceptance by the United States and Nicaragua of a customary principle which has universal applications. As to the content of the principle in customary law, the Court defines the constitutive elements which appear relevant in this case: a prohibited intervention must be one bearing on matters in which each State is permitted, by the principle of State sovereignty, to decide freely (for example the choice of a political, economic, social and cultural system, and formulation of foreign policy). Intervention is wrongful when it uses, in regard to such choices, methods of coercion, particularly force, either in the direct form of military action or in the indirect form of support for subversive activities in another State.

With regard to the practice of States, the Court notes that there have been in recent years a number of instances of foreign intervention in one State for the benefit of forces opposed to the government of that State. It concludes that the practice of States does not justify the view that any general right of intervention in support of an opposition within another State exists in contemporary international law; and this is in fact not asserted either by the United States or by Nicaragua.

4. Collective counter-measures in response to conduct not amounting to armed attack (paras. 210 and 211).

The Court then considers the question whether, if one State acts towards another in breach of the principle of non-intervention, a third State may lawfully take action by way of counter-measures which would amount to an intervention in the first State's internal affairs. This would be analogous to the right of self-defence in the case of armed attack, but the act giving rise to the reaction would be less grave, not amounting to armed attack. In the view of the Court, under international law in force today, States do not have a right of "collective" armed response to acts which do not constitute an "armed attack".

5. State sovereignty (paras. 212 to 214)

Turning to the principle of respect for State sovereignty, the Court recalls that the concept of sovereignty, both in treaty-law and in customary international law, extends to the internal waters and territorial sea of every State and to the airspace above its territory. It notes that the laying of mines necessarily affects the sovereignty of the coastal State, and that if the right of access to ports is hindered by the laying of mines by another State, what is infringed is the freedom of communications and of maritime commerce.

6. Humanitarian law (paras. 215 to 220)

The Court observes that the laying of mines in the waters of another State without any warning or notification is not only an unlawful act but also a breach of the principles of humanitarian law underlying the Hague Convention No.VIII of 1907. This consideration leads the Court on to examination of international humanitarian law applicable to the dispute. Nicaragua has not expressly invoked the provisions of international humanitarian law as such, but has complained of acts committed on its territory which would appear to be breaches thereof. In its submissions it has accused the United States of having killed, wounded and kidnapped citizens of Nicaragua. Since the evidence available is insufficient for the purpose of attributing to the United States the acts committed by the *contras*, the Court rejects this submission.

The question however remains of the law applicable to the acts of the United States in relation to the activities of the *contras*. Although Nicaragua has refrained from referring to the four Geneva Conventions of 12th August 1949, to which Nicaragua and the United States are parties, the Court considers that the rules stated in Article 3 which is common to the four Conventions, applying to armed conflicts of a non-international character, should be applied. The United States is under an obligation to "respect" the Conventions and even to "ensure respect" for them, and thus not to encourage persons or groups engaged in the conflict in Nicaragua to act in violation of the provisions of Article 3. This obligation derives from the general principles of humanitarian law to which the Conventions merely give specific expression.

7. The 1956 treaty (paras. 221 to 225)

In its Judgment of 26th November 1984, the Court concluded that it had jurisdiction to entertain claims concerning the existence of a dispute between the United States and Nicaragua as to the interpretation or application of a number of articles of the treaty of Friendship, Commerce and Navigation signed at Managua on 21st January 1956. It has to determine the meaning of the various relevant provisions, and in particular of Article XXI, paragraphs 1 (c) and 1 (d), by which the parties reserved the power to derogate from the other provisions.

XI. Application of the law to the facts (paras. 226 to 282)

Having set out the facts of the case and the rules of international law which appear to be in issue as a result of those facts, the Court has now to appraise the facts in relation to the legal rules applicable, and determine whether there are present any circumstances excluding the unlawfulness of particular acts.

1. The prohibition of the use of force and the right of self-defence (paras. 227 to 238)

Appraising the facts first in the light of the principle of the non-use of force, the Court considers that the laying of mines in early 1984 and certain attacks on Nicaraguan ports, oil installations and naval bases, imputable to the United States, constitute infringements of this principle, unless justified by circumstances which exclude their unlawfulness. It considers that the United States has committed a prima facie violation of the principle by arming and training the *contras*, unless this can be justified as an exercise of the right of self-defence.

On the other hand, it does not consider that military manoeuvres held by the United States near the Nicaraguan borders, or the supply of funds to the *contras*, amounts to a use of force.

The Court has to consider whether the acts which it regards as breaches of the principle may be justified by the exercise of the right of collective self-defence, and has therefore to establish whether the circumstances required are present. For this, it would first have to find that Nicaragua engaged in an armed attack against El Salvador, Honduras or Costa Rica, since only such an attack could justify reliance on the right of self-defence. As regards El Salvador, the Court considers that in customary international law the provision of arms to the opposition in another State does not constitute an armed attack on that State. As regards Honduras and Costa Rica, the Court states that, in the absence of sufficient information as to the transborder incursions into the territory of those two States from Nicaragua, it is difficult to decide whether they amount, singly or collectively, to an armed attack by Nicaragua. The Court finds that neither these incursions nor the alleged supply of arms may be relied on as justifying the exercise of the right of collective self-defence.

Secondly, in order to determine whether the United States was justified in exercising self-defence, the Court has to ascertain whether the circumstances required for the exercise of this right of collective self-defence were present, and therefore considers whether the States in question believed that they were the victims of an armed attack by Nicaragua, and requested the assistance of the United States in the exercise of collective self-defence. The Court has seen no evidence that the conduct of those States was consistent with such a situation.

Finally, appraising the United States activity in relation to the criteria of necessity and proportionality, the Court cannot find that the activities in question were undertaken in the light of necessity, and finds that some of them cannot be regarded as satisfying the criterion of proportionality.

Since the plea of collective self-defence advanced by the United States cannot be upheld, it follows that the United States has violated the principle prohibiting recourse to the threat or use of force by the acts referred to in the first paragraph of this section.

2. *The principle of non-intervention (paras. 239 to 245)*

The Court finds it clearly established that the United States intended, by its support of the *contras*, to coerce Nicaragua in respect of matters in which each State is permitted to decide freely, and that the intention of the *contras* themselves was to overthrow the present Government of Nicaragua. It considers that if one State, with a view to the coercion of another State, supports and assists armed bands in that State whose purpose is to overthrow its Government, that amounts to an intervention in its internal affairs, whatever the political objective of the State giving support. It therefore finds that the support given by the United States to the military and paramilitary activities of the *contras* in Nicaragua, by financial support, training, supply of weapons, intelligence and logistic support, constitutes a clear breach of the principle of non-intervention. Humanitarian aid on the other hand cannot be regarded as unlawful intervention. With effect from 1st October 1984, the United States Congress has restricted the use of funds to "humanitarian assistance" to the *contras*. The Court recalls that if the provision of "humanitarian assistance" is to escape condemnation as an intervention in the internal affairs of another State, it must be limited to the purposes hallowed in the practice of the Red Cross, and above all be given without discrimination.

With regard to the form of indirect intervention which Nicaragua sees in the taking of certain action of an economic nature against it by the United States, the Court is unable to regard such action in the present case as a breach of the customary law principle of non-intervention.

3. *Collective counter-measures in response to conduct not amounting to armed attack (paras. 246 to 249)*

Having found that intervention in the internal affairs of another State does not produce an entitlement to take collective counter-measures involving the use of force, the Court finds that the acts of which Nicaragua is accused, even assuming them to have been established and imputable to that State, could not justify counter-measures taken by a third State, the United States, and particularly could not justify intervention involving the use of force.

4. *State sovereignty (paras. 250 to 253)*

The Court finds that the assistance to the contras, the direct attacks on Nicaraguan ports, oil installations, etc., the mining operations in Nicaraguan ports, and the acts of intervention involving the use of force referred to in the Judgment, which are already a breach of the principle of non-use of force, are also an infringement of the principle of respect for territorial sovereignty. This principle is also directly infringed by the unauthorized overflight of Nicaraguan territory. These acts cannot be justified by the activities in El Salvador attributed to Nicaragua; assuming that such activities did in fact occur, they do not bring into effect any right belonging to the United States. The Court also concludes that, in the context of the present proceedings, the laying of mines in our near Nicaraguan ports constitutes an infringement, to Nicaragua's detriment, of the freedom of communications and of maritime commerce.

5. *Humanitarian law (paras. 254 to 256)*

The Court has found the United States responsible for the failure to give notice of the mining of Nicaraguan ports.

It has also found that, under general principles of humanitarian law, the United States was bound to refrain from encouragement of persons or groups engaged in the conflict in Nicaragua to commit violations of common Article 3 of the four Geneva Conventions of 12th August 1949. The manual on "Psychological Operations in Guerrilla Warfare", for the publication and dissemination of which the United States is responsible, advises certain acts which cannot but be regarded as contrary to that article.

6. *Other grounds mentioned in justification of the acts of the United States (paras. 257 to 269)*

The United States has linked its support to the *contras* with alleged breaches by the Government of Nicaragua of certain solemn commitments to the Nicaraguan people, the United States and the OAS. The Court considers whether there is anything in the conduct of Nicaragua which might legally warrant counter-measures by the United States in response to the alleged violations. With reference to the "Plan to secure peace" put forward by the Junta of the Government of National Reconstruction (12th July 1979), the Court is unable to find anything in the documents and communications transmitting the plan from which it can be inferred that any legal undertaking was intended to exist. The Court cannot contemplate the creation of a new rule opening up a right of intervention by one State against another on the ground that the latter has opted for some particular ideology or political system. Furthermore the Respondent has not advanced a legal argument based on an alleged new principle of "ideological convention".

With regard more specifically to alleged violations of human rights relied on by the United States, the Court considers that the use of force by the United States could not be the appropriate method to monitor or ensure respect for such rights, normally provided for in the applicable conventions. With regard to the alleged militarization of Nicaragua, also referred to by the United States to justify its activities, the Court observes that in international law there are no rules, other than such rules as may be accepted by the State concerned, by treaty or otherwise, whereby the level of armaments of a sovereign State can be limited, and this principle is valid for all States without exception.

7. The 1956 Treaty (paras. 270 to 282)

The Court turns to the claim of Nicaragua based on the Treaty of Friendship, Commerce and Navigation of 1956, and the claim that the United States has deprived the Treaty of its object and purpose and emptied it of real content. The Court cannot however entertain these claims unless the conduct complained of is not "measures...necessary to protect the essential security interests" of the United States, since Article XXI of the Treaty provides that the Treaty shall not preclude the application of such measures. With regard to the question what activities of the United States might have been such as to deprive the Treaty of its object and purpose, the Court makes a distinction. It is unable to regard all the acts complained of in that light, but considers that there are certain activities which undermine the whole spirit of the agreement. These are the mining of Nicaraguan ports, the direct attacks on ports, oil installations, etc., and the general trade embargo.

The Court also upholds the contention that the mining of the ports is in manifest contradiction with the freedom of navigation and commerce guaranteed by Article XIX of the Treaty. It also concludes that the trade embargo proclaimed on 1st May 1985 is contrary to that article.

The Court therefore finds that the United States is prima facie in breach of an obligation not to deprive the 1956 Treaty of its object and purpose (*pacta sunt servanda*), and has committed acts in contradiction with the terms of the Treaty. The Court has however to consider whether the exception in Article XXI concerning "measures...necessary to protect the essential security interests" of a Party may be invoked to justify the acts complained of. After examining the available material, particularly the Executive Order of President Reagan of 1st May 1985, the Court finds that the mining of Nicaraguan ports, and the direct attacks on ports and oil installations, and the general trade embargo of 1st May 1985, cannot be justified as necessary to protect the essential security interests of the United States.

XII. The claim for reparation (paras. 283 to 285)

The court is requested to adjudge and declare that compensation is due to Nicaragua, the quantum thereof to be fixed subsequently, and to award to Nicaragua the sum of 370.2 million US dollars as an interim award. After satisfying itself that it has jurisdiction to order reparation, the Court considers appropriate the request of Nicaragua for the nature and amount of the reparation to be determined in a subsequent phase of the proceedings. It also considers that there is no provision in the Statute of the Court either specifically empowering it or debarring it from making an interim award of the kind requested. In a case in which one Party is not appearing, the Court should refrain from any unnecessary act which might prove an obstacle to a negotiated settlement. The Court therefore does not consider that it can accede *at this stage* to this request by Nicaragua.

XIII. The provisional measures (paras. 286 to 289)

After recalling certain passages in its Order of 10th May 1984, the Court concludes that it is incumbent on each Party not to direct its conduct solely by reference to what it believes to be its rights. Particularly is this so in a situation of armed conflict where no reparation can efface the results of conduct which the Court may rule to have been contrary to international law.

XIV. Peaceful settlement of disputes; the Contadora process (paras. 290 to 291)

In the present case the Court has already taken note of the Contadora process, and of the fact that it had been endorsed by the United Nations Security Council and General Assembly, as well as by Nicaragua and the United States. It recalls to both Parties to the present case the need to co-operate with the Contadora efforts in seeking a definitive and lasting peace in Central America, in accordance with the principle of customary international law that prescribes the peaceful settlement of international disputes, also endorsed by Article 33 of the United Nations Charter.

The Debate on Detente I: Peace and Freedom as Objects of Detente

Horst Ehmke

Professor Dr. Horst
Ehmke is Deputy
Chairman of the SPD
Bundestag Parliamentary
Party and a member of
the SPD Party Executive.
This article is published
in the Festschrift for
Eugen Selbmann, under
the title Twenty Years of
East Policy.

A conflict which deserves the greatest attention has broken out in the European peace movement. Under the slogan "Against detente from above, all for a detente from below", one of the fundamental themes of the seventies' discussion about policy towards the East is under review. It is the question of the relationship of peace *with* the Eastern bloc, and of peace *within* that bloc in the context of our policy towards those countries.

The conflict in the peace movement may be outlined as follows: some participants appreciate the Social Democrats' detente but now think that a new impulse is necessary; others reject such a policy as "detente from above" through negotiations and agreements with the Communist authorities in the East. Instead, they demand "detente from below" through the activities of peace movements in West and East. However, a "peace movement from the grass-roots" will clash with the authorities of Communist countries.

Ton Veerkamp is a member of the peace movement and university chaplain in West Berlin. He has tried to use the example of the Interchurch Peace Council (IKV) of the Netherlands as a model for these developments. IKV is one of the most influential groups of the West European peace movement. In order to exert influence on the government's decisions about the missiles, IKV has been obliged to demonstrate not only their competence but also their credibility. In doing so, IKV had to defend itself against a campaign from the Right that claimed its activities would serve the interests of Moscow. IKV answered this slander by saying that disarmament in the West would not only deprive the East of an argument for its own arms programme, but also of the excuse for suppressing freedom of speech in the Eastern bloc. The growth of the peace movement also serves the development of freedom in the East, — Solidarnosc in Poland, for example. When Solidarnosc was suppressed in December

1981, IKV compounded its basic error — that of making its own credibility conditional on the behaviour of the Communist regimes — into a system. Solidarnosc, Charter 77, and such groups were designated the natural allies of the Western peace movement. "Detente from above" had failed; "detente from below" demands freedom of development for the opposition in the Eastern bloc (as well as the West), and consequently the step-by-step demolition of the Eastern internal political systems.

As a consequence of this "policy", Veerkamp asserted that parts of the peace movement were no longer looked upon as serious interlocuters by the political powers in the East constituted by the Communist parties. "Detente from below" was no real policy, merely a morally excited reaction to these reflections of the East. It would achieve even less than "detente from above" could be claimed to have done.

Veerkamp's criticism of this tendency should be taken still further; for it runs the risk of seriously hindering detente as it drives the Communist parties in the opposite direction. It also adds to the illegality of the peace and protest groups in the Eastern bloc. Furthermore, it is in practice impossible to sustain the artificial contrast between "detente from above" and "detente from below". The assumption that, over the heads of governments in East and West, it would be possible to conjure up a European peace system on a democratic basis, is misplaced. Peace policy needs action by governments and parliaments, as well as the mobilization of people. In the Federal German Republic (FRG) we can observe the differences there are in relation to detente between a social democratic and a conservative government. On the other hand, the SPD has to learn a lesson. As a party of government, it ought not to neglect society's formation of a moral sense through peace activities amongst the citizenry. Social Democrats' co-operation in the work of the peace movement is a duty of trust.

Critical reflection upon this discussion in the peace movement leads me to conclude that the tendency described earlier springs less from overconfidence in the people and more from internal uncertainty. As an anti-missiles movement and a "single issue" pressure group, the peace movement has clearly suffered a defeat. Now it wishes to overcome its present limitations by developing a broader political concept which has more mileage. Its turning to the dissident groups in Eastern Europe should be assessed in relation to two points: its relations with the domestic political parties of the Right — which slander it — and its relation to the Communism established in the Eastern bloc as a factor of foreign policy.

To start with, let's consider the peace movement's relations with the domestic political Right. The charge of "serving Moscow" has been raised not only against the peace movement's activities, but also against the policy of the German Social Democrats. The Interchurch Peace Council (IKV) in the Netherlands knows as well as we do that it is not the avowal of democracy and human rights that is at issue. Rather, the problem is the "tradition" of political parties of the Right distorting questions of foreign policy towards the communist states by slanderously exploiting them as a cudgel in domestic political debates. Up until now, the German Union parties have committed this slander at every federal election. It will not be otherwise in 1987.

Although anti-communism is deeply rooted in the consciousness and sub-consciousness of our nation, (not to mention the democratic rejection of all totalitarian systems, partly on account of 12 years of Nazi propaganda, but especially because of the experience of the Red Army occupation), in their discussions with the Eastern bloc the Social Democrats have never descended to the cheap platitudes of the Right. In their discussions with the Communists and the hyper-dogmatism of Marxism-Leninism, the Social Democrats dispose of far more experience than all the Conservatives put together, starting with the division of the labour movement through to the enforced union of the Socialists and the Communists in the Eastern zone. The Right's non-adaptation is a decisive inhibition not only to effective discussion with the Communists, but also to the continually renewed study of peace policy that is necessary for providing a viable and sensitive public opinion.

The second aspect, that of the relation to the established Communism of the Eastern bloc as a factor of foreign policy, is far more complicated. In analysing Soviet politics and in our own policy towards the Soviet Union, we should always take account of two factors at once: power and ideology. As we have said, in their discussions with the Eastern bloc the Social Democrats have never resorted to the cheap platitudes of the Right, exploiting democratic rejection of totalitarian systems. Do certain parts of the West European peace movement really feel at home with such forces from the Right? Strange bedfellows!

The difficult aspects of our relationship to established Communism as a factor of foreign policy become clear if considered in the light of the wish for peace with the Eastern bloc. Freedom in the Eastern bloc within the objective of a policy of detente also becomes clear when examined in this light. The main object of that policy is to achieve a real state of peace in Europe. According to the Social Democrats, this objective should be achieved by developing a partnership of security between East and West, notwithstanding their different social systems. It has been made plain to those on the Right that detente between countries, or even their "co-existence", could in no way put a stop to ideological discussion or the peaceful rivalry of the two social systems.

Partnership between countries will always be endangered by hostility (instead of mere contrast) between social systems and detente policy. With regard to power and ideology, actions put pressure upon internal political and ideological development and the domestic dimension of detente in Europe. Relations to the dissident groups in the East must be the subject of the argument on peace policy. For that reason, the Social Democrats should accept the discussion within the peace movement with much self-criticism.

Although the results of the Social Democrats' detente policy are indisputable, unquestionably things got stuck in the 1980s, and this represented a decline. However, the reasons for this state of affairs are less likely to be found in the compass of ideological rivalry than in that of the superpowers. I see the faltering of detente policy as the responsibility of the superpowers.

Firstly, the self-renewing dynamism of the arms race has been underestimated. The presumption that a reduction of political stress would not only lead to regular co-operation, but in the end somehow "automatically" engender a decrease in armaments, has overlooked the point that armaments are not simply a consequence but nowadays one of the main causes of the stress which we are facing. Detente policy and increasing armaments have co-existed for years, but it has become clear that detente policy in the form of arms control and disarmament must make an impact also in the military sphere, otherwise it would fail.

The dynamism of the arms race not only expresses at once and in both systems the dynamics of the military-industrial complexes, but also the dynamics of the interests of the superpowers. For instance, the superpowers are not merely pursuing their interests with all the means at their disposal in their own "backyards" of Afghanistan, Nicaragua, and Grenada. In sharp contrast with their obligation under international law, they fail to comply with the non-proliferation treaty concerning nuclear weapons. In order to assert their superpower interests worldwide, they do not shrink from open confrontation without any consideration of the interests of smaller countries.

For that reason those countries are faced with the question of how best to assert their own interests through serious new efforts towards detente and arms control, rather than simply following the reflexes of the superpowers. For the Social Democrats, security partnership and the maintenance of Europe's identity are policies which belong together as a second phase of the East, or more correctly, the West-East policy.

In addition, the power factors which have acted as a brake on detente policy in the 1970s are interlinked with ideological ones. For example, for the Soviet Union Eastern Europe is not only a security and political fortification gained at the cost of great sacrifices during World War II; it also marked the end of a long isolation for the Soviet Union as the only socialist country. It was an important development in the "socialist world-system of states." On the other hand, for the West the division of Europe is not only a question of peace but also one of human rights. An example of this outside Europe was when the Red Army marched into the buffer state of Afghanistan. This was a continuation of the expansionist policy of the tsarist era, but at the same time an action of "proletarian internationalism", a response of international solidarity with all socialist regimes by the Soviet Union. Conversely, for the USA their barely concealed military intervention in Central America and their open intervention in Grenada do not only represent the exercise of power. It is a question of fighting, or at least containing, subversive ideologies in that region.

The difficult aspects of our relationship to established Communism as a factor of foreign policy in the Eastern bloc becomes clearer if looked at in the light of the desire for peace in the Eastern bloc. Freedom within the Eastern bloc and within the objective of a policy of detente also becomes more evident when examined in this light. The main objective of that policy is the achievement of a real state of peace in Europe. This goal ought to be reached, according to the Social Democrats, by developing a security partnership between East and West, notwithstanding their different social systems. For this reason, the Right ought to know that detente between countries, or even their "co-existence", could in no way put a stop to the ideological discussion or the peaceful rivalry of the two social systems.

Partnership between countries will always be endangered by hostility (instead of mere contrast) of the social systems and detente policy. And in relationship to the inter-mingling of power and ideology, actions put pressure upon the internal political and ideological development and the internal dimension of detente in Europe. Its relationship with the dissidents' groups in the East must also be part of the arguments about peace policy. The Social Democrats should therefore consider the discussion in the peace movement self-critically.

Notwithstanding this mixture of power and ideology, and in spite of the stability of the socio-political faiths on both sides, the obstruction of detente by ideological differences has been much smaller than some in the peace movement believe. Above all we should bear in mind that the basic ideological question at the start of detente was not whether the Eastern bloc could cope with the ideological and the domestic political effects of detente. At the beginning, the anxiety of many conservatives in the West was whether detente might be a Trojan horse carrying communism and world revolution in its belly, into the Federal Republic and Western Europe.

At the time, the Social Democrats maintained that there was no reason to fear contact with, or feel any sense of inferiority towards, the Communists. Democrats should, and could, readily take the lead in discussion with Communists and show self-confidence about the peaceful rivalry of the social systems. Developments have proved them right.

During the years of detente, the Communist parties in Western Europe, including that of West Germany, have grown weaker rather than stronger. Economic crisis, with high levels of long-term unemployed, has not reversed this trend. The Communists, including the German Communists, have exerted a certain influence on the peace movement, but this has neither ameliorated their poor electoral performance, nor has it led to their domination of the peace movement. Moreover, in Western Europe a development started by de-Stalinization (itself initiated by Khrushchev and confirmed by the 20th Congress of the Communist Party of the Soviet Union) has evolved into a reformist Communism. Its development has found its most remarkable expression in the "Eurocommunism" of the Italian Communists under Enrico Berlinguer. In the autumn of 1976 at a conference in East Berlin, the Yugoslav, Italian, and Spanish Communists successfully vindicated the right of their countries and that of any country to their "own road to socialism" against the Comintern tradition of World Communism governed by Moscow.

Today, contrary to the promise held out by Communism, the fact that wars are also carried on between socialist states causes widespread international repercussions and disillusionment, just as disclosure of the crimes committed by Stalin has done internally. This is one of the reasons why the Comintern tradition of world revolution has lost part of its attraction and influence in Europe and the Third World. The Soviet Union, having profited less by the de-colonization after World War Two than might have been expected, has as a consequence of its invasion of Afghanistan damaged decisively the credibility of its policy in the Third World. For the latter, Chinese Communism is more attractive nowadays, since it has solved the food problem for the most populated developing country, whereas the Soviet Union, 70 years after the October Revolution, is still obliged to import cereals.

Outside the Soviet Union and the Eastern bloc Moscow's ideological influence has grown weaker rather than stronger during the era of detente. In the meantime, there arises the question of whether the ideological effects of detente policy in the Eastern bloc could possibly cause a divergence from Moscow Communism. In my opinion, this question should also be answered in the negative. But it is a very complicated issue.

From the beginning of detente it has been obvious that the social interest in that policy did not spring exclusively from the security or political concerns of the Eastern bloc. Nor did it spring from peace and maintenance of the territorial status quo, born as a consequence of Hitler's war. Co-operation with the West was expected by the Soviet Union to help compensate for its deficiencies, in that it is only militarily equal to the USA, not economically or technologically. In addition, the Soviet Union hoped for a contribution to the internal stabilization of the East European countries by means of raised living standards, as a consequence of co-operation with the West. Thus, for the Soviet Union and the other Eastern bloc countries detente has from the beginning also had an internal dimension.

If we wish to appreciate fully the domestic political effects of detente in the Eastern bloc, we must consider two facts. Firstly, the difficulties the Soviet Union encounters over the stabilization of the internal situation in Eastern Europe are not a consequence of detente. They are a consequence of the co-ordination of these states during the Cold War, a co-ordination made possible by eliminating national Communist forces. This was demonstrated by the rebellions in the German Democratic Republic, Hungary, Poland, and during the "Prague Spring", which all took place during the 1950s and 1960s, coinciding with the start of detente.

Secondly, we must recognise clearly that detente can by no means shift the Soviet Union's determination under all circumstances to maintain their glacis in Eastern Europe achieved during the Second World War. This has been demonstrated by the Warsaw Pact invasion of Czechoslovakia in 1968 and the proclamation of martial law in Poland in 1981. The important difference was that in Poland, unlike in Prague in 1968, no Soviet troops became involved. The two Soviet divisions stationed in the country stayed in barracks. This difference should be attributed not only to detente but also to Poland's special internal situation. But it does not alter the reality.

The experience has also confirmed that a policy of destabilization of the

Eastern bloc could neither serve detente nor peace. Although the question of the internal political effects of detente in the Eastern bloc is by no means exhausted by this consideration, the scope for such developments is clearly defined.

It is common knowledge that the domestic situations of the different East European states are very different. For example, we may contrast Hungary and Romania. However, we have come to realise through witnessing the nearby example of the German Democratic Republic (GDR), that the regimes in the East have coped on the whole amazingly well with detente, both in respect to domestic politics and ideologically. This applies in the GDR, although this state is not at all sure of its ground in a divided Germany, as is also shown by the "refined" frontier regime. The notion of an intensive interchange with the East in the fields of economy, science, and culture and a million visitors a year from West Germany may originally have caused nightmares in the security organs about the poisoning of East Germans by the bacillus of "social democracy". Nowadays the heads of government in the GDR not only tolerate the reception of West German television, they even transmit it through their own cable network, establishing the networks in regions where the reception via aerials is not possible. This change of attitude has been occasioned not only by the fact that the "Golden West" has now lost much of its former glory (economic crisis and mass unemployment have supplanted economic wonder), or that satellite television will somehow revolutionize reception possibilities. The decisive factor seems to be that the opening which orginated in the detente period is clearly in the interest of the regime. This opening may on the one hand increase demand for foreign travel, and on the other lead to bolder and more open criticism by the growing numbers of dissidents and peace groups. "Swords into ploughshares" also serves as an opening, and has become especially clear in the GDR. Here, in Erich Honecker, we see, if not the legitimation, then somehow a more tractable acceptance of political leaders.

This limited internal political opening, including loosening the monopoly on information, is evidently also being directed towards the integration of criticism and opposition. Other approaches applied are tying the population to the regime, and improvements in the opportunities for discussion for political staff. After all, as yet the GDR is not as far forward as the Hungarians and the Poles who now can choose, if not yet between two parties then between alternative candidates.

What is the basis for the stabilizing internal political effect of detente in the Eastern bloc? First of all, it is based on a detente policy which even in the East conforms to the wish of all peoples for peace. This applies especially to the peoples of the Soviet Union within whose memory the experience of war with its terrible sacrifices is deeply imprinted. The manifold problems the Eastern bloc face can only be solved in conditions of peace.

Furthermore, not only the governments but also the peoples of Eastern Europe welcome the refrain from the use of force and the respect of the territorial status quo which has developed in consequence of the war against Hitler. Anybody who acts as if adherence to the inviolability of Poland's western frontier is merely the position of a Communist is deceiving themselves as well as others, especially those who were expelled. It is at the same time a concern of the whole Polish nation, including the Roman Catholic Church and Solidarnosc. In addition, the desire for a rise in living standards through economic co-operation with the West is not merely the aspiration of the Communist leaders but also of the peoples in Eastern Europe. The economic, scientific, and cultural interchange with the West relieves their isolation, creates free spaces, and strengthens the consciousness of the historical and cultural solidarity of the Europeans.

The peoples of Eastern Europe know perfectly well that detente has widened a little the scope of their states and has allowed a cautious opening up internally. As revealed by the comparison of Hungary with Romania, there are indeed important differences in the use of that space. However, this does not at all alter the basic experience: "cold war" and superpower confrontation in Europe have precipitated both the "iron curtain" and a stringent "iron" bloc discipline, while detente policy has led to a partial phasing out of "enemy" images and to the loosening up of the regimes.

The lack of an exact analysis of the domestic situation in a historical context in the East European countries has drawn many in the West to the false conclusion that the people's aspiration for improvement of their position implies a desire for a union with the West. This is a misunderstanding. After their experiences with Hitler's Germany, many non-Communists in Eastern Europe also subscribe, for example, to the view that security for their countries can only be achieved by relying on the Soviet Union. Nor are they very much inclined to return to the pre-war regimes, least of all those of fascist origin. They, as well as the dissident groups, do not hanker for a return to a society dominated by capitalist property and power relations.

What counts with the peoples of Eastern Europe, on whose behalf the dissidents are acting, is respect for their human rights as well as for their individual and political freedom. The dissidents are claiming these rights and not only for their children. They are claiming most of them without any restictions whatsoever as their goal. "Freedom is indivisible", as we read during the "Prague Spring". Such a demand for "all or nothing" is unrealizable under the Communist government. It would amount to the Soviet Union's surrender of itself and of its East European glacis. Whoever in the West promises the peoples of Eastern Europe a clean sweep of the regime by pressure from the outside or from below, is only damaging their cause for propaganda purposes.

Does this mean that the dissidents are morally in the wrong? Certainly not! It is important for Social Democrats to realize this fact whenever, from their safe Western bulwark, they advise the peoples of Eastern Europe to be patient and realistic. But on the other hand, excessive moralising — however well meant — can only lead to a political disaster. What we have to account for, including to the dissidents in Eastern Europe, are not our good sentiments but the consequences of our policies.

Does this mean that instead of a policy of "destabilizing" we should pursue a policy of "stabilizing" the Communist status quo in the East European countries? Surely not. How could we act against our own democratic conviction and against the hopes of the peoples of Eastern Europe? The inner dimension of detente can neither be called "destabilization" nor "stabilization". It is called "reform". If consensus could be reached on this subject, much would have been gained.

This leads us to the question of whether the Communist regimes are capable of reform in respect of human rights and political freedom. This is meant not in the sense that reforms are inevitable or irreversible, but in the sense that they cannot simply be excluded. This question cannot be answered *a priori*. During the past decade there has been a loosening of the Eastern bloc regimes. This can be seen in the period of detente from the de-Stalinization under Khrushchev through to the openings in the East European countries. Can we already conclude that this trend demonstrates an elementary capacity for reform? A study of totalitarianism in the postwar period answers this question chiefly in the negative, both for Communism and for National Socialism. Indeed, the crimes of the Stalin era do not appear in a better light on account of their having been committed as a perversity of European tradition and in the name of ideals. But with respect to the capacity for reform, is there not a certain difference to be observed between the perversion of humanist ideals and the degrading principles of National Socialism?

It is at any rate difficult to imagine a 'Helsinki' process of the Western powers and a discussion on human rights with Nazi Germany. In our opinion, the important achievement of the Helsinki agreement lies in the fact that today in Europe discussions are in progress between East and West and between democratic and Communist social systems about human rights. Everyone who tries to make human rights a propaganda weapon in the discussion with the East endangers the only process by which a long-term improvement in human rights in the Eastern bloc can be achieved.

Apart from that, we should not pretend that on human rights only the East is at fault. Questions to the West, for example on the right to work or of the equality of rights of races and sexes, cannot be wished away as mere impertinence. We are still far from the "economic liberation of the moral and political person", as Kurt Schumacher once described the purpose of socialism. This is shown once again by the present crises in capitalist society with its mass unemployment. The West also badly needs reform!

When asserting the capacity for reform of the Communist regimes, a distinction has to be made between the Soviet Union and the states of Eastern Europe with respect to their development. More than in the Soviet Union, in the East European states national history and the whole European tradition are important influences towards reform.

By wanting to secure at any price its East European glacis, the Soviet Union has experienced what Talleyrand described in the following terms; "You can do all kinds of things with bayonets, but you can't sit on them." The Soviet Union will therefore need to consider whether "reforms instead of armour" should perhaps be the catchword and the solution for political

58

stabilization in Eastern Europe. And even when such reforms do not lead to a "Finlandization" of the East European states, the Finnish example does show that even extensive loosening of the Eastern bloc regimes need not necessarily damage the security and political interests of the Soviet Union.

Detente is justified by the mere fact that it pursues peace between the states of East and West (with the prospect of good results) while the ideological and social differences and contrasts remain. However, since the relationships within states cannot be separated simply from the relationship between states (from the social systems and detente necessarily affecting the ideological and inner political development of both), detente's inner dimension ought to be realized in such a way that it has a positive influence on the conditions for reform.

The Debate on Detente II: The Politics of Detente and Human Rights

Mient Jan Faber

Mient Jan Faber is Secretary of the Interchurch Peace Council (IKV) in the Netherlands.

For some time now, the student pastor, Ton Veerkamp, has been conducting a crusade against the peace movement; at least against that part of the movement which identifies itself with the Interchurch Peace Council (IKV) in the Netherlands.[1] What his position comes down to is that IKV has succumbed to right-wing elements in Dutch society. Since 1977, IKV has been conducting a campaign with the slogan, "Help rid the world of nuclear weapons, let it begin in the Netherlands." The struggle against deployment of cruise missiles is one aspect of this campaign. According to Veerkamp, this campaign has stirred up so much criticism from rightists — that IKV is one-sided, that it understimates the threat in and from the Eastern bloc, that it is an agent of Moscow — that IKV is now suffering from a credibility crisis. In order to win back the confidence of its own population, still in Veerkamp's words, IKV has charted a new route. After the military take-over in Poland on 13th December 1981, IKV declared its solidarity with Solidarnosc and with all kinds of other so-called "independent" groups in Eastern Europe, such as Charter 77 in Czechoslovakia. These groups were declared the "natural allies" in the struggle against the bloc system, which in turn was branded as the cause of the arms race and many other evils. This was how IKV responded to the "criticism from the Right". At the moment, the policy of IKV can be reduced to the principle, if we stick to Veerkamp's line of reasoning, that the price that Eastern European (Warsaw Pact) countries must pay for the existence of peace movements such as IKV is to make their political systems conform to the Western model.

Veerkamp, of Dutch descent and now a minister in Berlin, has managed to make a name for himself in the Federal Republic as a knowledgeable informant about IKV. However, he has apparently viewed the Netherlands with too Berlin-tinted eyes. In any case, he has neglected to study seriously what IKV has said and written about Eastern Europe, human rights, and the issue of peace. But his critique is more than a misunderstanding in the sense that his image of Europe is different from mine. For Veerkamp, the Soviet Union has been the whipping boy of Europe (1918-1921 and 1941-1945), and an incredible amount of suffering was inflicted upon Russian Communists and the people of the Soviet Union.

What he says about the suffering of the Russians is true, but I was inclined to leave his argument for what it was until he carelessly included the Dutch people in Hitler's SS gangs that went into Russia. In numerous Dutch families, including my own, there is still much undigested suffering which was inflicted upon them by the Nazis. It seems as if Veerkamp needs such offensive arguments in order to put the finishing touches to his ideology. The Soviet Union against the rest, two fundamentally different forms of human civilisation; and from reading Veerkamp, one gets the impression that ours hardly deserves the name civilisation. The peace movement, according to Veerkamp, denies that there is any sort of human civilisation in Eastern Europe. It has put itself in the camp with the reactionaries, with J.Foster Dulles and his roll-back theory. It feels comfortable with Reagan's statement that the Soviet Union represents the Evil Empire, barbarism.

I would have saved myself the trouble of dealing with Veerkamp's articles, were it not that he apparently enjoys a certain amount of authority in SPD circles. In fact, no less than Prof. Dr. Horst Ehmke, acting chair of the SPD in parliament, uses Veerkamp's analysis as the foundation for his argument in *Die Neue Gesellschaft, Frankfurter Hefte II* in which he defends and explains his Party's position regarding the politics of detente, peace, and freedom.[2] Thus he carelessly copies the idea that IKV (and therefore the peace movement) has rejected *Entspannungspolitik von oben* (detente from above) — negotiating and concluding agreements with the Communist powers in the East — and has, in its place, insisted on *Entspannungspolitik van unten* (detente from below) — the building of contacts between civil societies in the East and West. The term "civil society" originated in Hungary and refers to that part of society outside the governmental and party apparatus. According to Ehmke, in an attempt to justify its one-sided campaign, IKV claims that disarmament in the West will have a positive effect on the amount of space for action and freedom of expression in the East. This "fundamental mistake" was even developed into a "system" — Ehmke has appropriated the terminology from Veerkamp — after Solidarnosc was defeated in December 1981. The result was that official contacts with political organs in the East were seriously hindered because these Eastern European agencies had, of course, little use for a Western peace movement intent on destabilizing East European regimes. What remained then for IKV was self-overestimation and empty boasting — that is how Ehmke developed Veerkamp's position to its logical conclusion. You cannot reasonably expect that a European peace order could be reached by working around those who now have the political power in East and West, by following the path of grassroots democracy. Or, to put it more crudely, because of its destabilizing character, this detente from below will ultimately lead to a liquidation of peace and detente policy.

It is unfortunate that Ehmke did not take the trouble to examine more closely what he calls IKV's "fundamental mistake". His own article is even based on it. Ehmke, namely, not only claims that the "new cold war" in Europe is the result of the superpowers' arms policies — that is exactly what IKV proposes — but then he also makes a great effort to prove that it is precisely the SPD's policy of detente that has contributed to a broadening of elbow room in Eastern Europe in terms of both external and internal affairs. The latter (internal affairs) is in the form of more openness and possibilities for their citizens in numerous fields of activity. I do not see how this could be anything other than what IKV "claims".

The problem is that Ehmke is not aware of what the real issues are that divide IKV and the SPD. That comes from relying on the wrong spokespersons. In my opinion, our differences of opinion are not related to our judgement of the first phase of *Ostpolitik*[3] but derive from some other issues, namely:

— what is the special role of the civil sector as opposed to the political sector of society?; and

— given our understanding of the role of the civil sector, what should then be the characteristic of the policy of detente?

Before going into these points, let me first give a sketch of the line followed by IKV.

Although IKV has had formal ties with the church since 1966, it has worked independently on issues of war and peace. Since 1977, IKV has functioned as a sort of political organisation. In that year it decided to create a power-base for the ideas that were developed. This power-base was in the form of a campaign — a democratic organisation with chapters throughout the country. The slogan given to the campaign was, "Help rid the world of nuclear weapons, let it begin in the Netherlands". An important reason for beginning this campaign against nuclear and conventional arms was to sustain the *policy of detente*. With great esteem and approval, to this very day, we have spread reports of successes mainly achieved by Social Democratic efforts for detente (Brandt, Schmidt). In our opinion, in the mid-1970s the policies of detente were endangered by the upcoming round of modernisation in the field of nuclear weapons, and the lack of agreements and treaties which could have brought the arms build-up to a halt. That is why we began to emphasize European initiatives — given our situation, we particularly suggested *West* European initiatives — that could tighten the reins on the superpowers, and, more specifically, we issued pleas for independent measures by individual countries (inside the alliances). That explains the phrase, "to begin in the Netherlands". IKV is not now and never was in favour of unilateral (nuclear) disarmament, but hoped to be able to stimulate a process that could lead to more involvement and real acts which would result in the maintenance of peace, further detente, and closer relations between East and West. As a social organisation, we appealed to public opinion using our power-base as a spring-board to pressure "policies". One result was the long (six years) Dutch hesitation to agree to the deployment of cruise missiles. This contrasted with the other deployment countries which all punctually followed the deployment schedule. We also addressed ourselves to churches and other like-minded organisations in East and West, asking for understanding and support for our approach. It is true that in these circles full support was given to a wide variety of ideas which in Western Europe were directed towards the struggle against the double-track decision of NATO, but they did not distil into a coherent political approach to the issues of peace and security. A serious obstacle was that the peace movements in most of the countries were poorly organised and had insufficient personnel, and were even often no more than ad hoc coalitions of groups which had more than merely "peace" in their portfolios.

In Eastern Europe contacts were built up with churches, with the officially-recognised peace councils, but also with those who occupied themselves with the issue of peace in an independent way, such as Charter 77. In both the West and the East, IKV followed its own double-track policy. *Track one* was directed towards the *civil sector*: the maintenance and development of contacts and discussions about peace and security with social institutions, groups, and individuals. *Track two* was directed towards the political sector: discussions with and the influencing of political parties, governments, and their organs in order to promote the desired changes.

It goes without saying that we were aware of the differing political systems in Eastern and Western Europe. Our point of departure, however, was that a civil sector is present in all of the countries of Europe over which, on the one hand, the political systems exercise their power, but from which, on the other hand, the political forces derive their authority. With a minimum of support and legitimation from the population, it is, after all, difficult to exercise rule in human civilization.

In this manner our broad approach should serve two purposes:

a) to intensify the process of detente;

b) to bring the arms race to an end.

The claim that IKV landed in a credibility crisis because of its "one-sided" proposals and finally gave way to criticism from the Right is, however, as nicely as it has been represented, completely in conflict with reality. I explained above that our policy was not narrowly oriented to our country with the idea, "Let's try to get nuclear weapons out of the Netherlands and who cares about what happens in the rest of Europe." When the "Right" accuses us of such an attitude, we always answered them reasonably, and when that turned out to be impossible we just turned our backs on them. Getting down on our knees for the right wing is something that IKV has never done.

This may be difficult to understand for someone like Veerkamp, who lives in a situation where slander is a serious factor to be reckoned with, but the right wing campaign of slander against IKV, that it got its orders from Moscow, was more amusing than upsetting for us. It did not last even three months. By the end of September 1981 it had passed, after the Dutch Minister of Foreign Affairs declared before the Parliament that such accusations were not supported by the slightest trace of evidence, neither "hard" nor "soft". Consequently, this took place considerably before the events of December in Poland which, according to Veerkamp, so greatly influenced the "fundamental mistake" and the "salto mortale" of IKV: striving for internal change of the Eastern opposition, at a time when it did not appear possible to exercise any real influence on Dutch politics. Again, isn't that "fundamental mistake" nothing more than what any broad-minded political movement wants, namely to exercise a favourable influence (marginal as it may be) on the international political context. The fact that after December 1981 IKV began to talk more and more about the question of whether the changes in Eastern Europe were desirable and obtainable, had nothing to do with a reaction to the right wing.

There was no real "credibility crisis" instigated by the right wing in the Netherlands. For IKV it was simply the result of our *own* need to show how the things which we demanded for Dutch politics could have an international effect. It is true that at that time we hoped that the importance which the Soviet Union attached to a strong peace movement in the West would also have some influence on their hesitation to interfere in Poland. We knew that this would not be the decisive factor, but we thought that Moscow's loss of power in Poland would be answered by an equal loss of power in the West — less cohesion (more pluriformity) in NATO because the double-track decision would have been upset. Anyway, no matter how you view this line of reasoning, putting Dulles' roll-back and Reagan's pressure politics on an equal footing shows a considerable lack of understanding. Ehmke's vision of looking after European interests inside NATO — arms control together with detente — comes much closer to what IKV had and has in mind.

As already stated, East-West relations and detente have been at the forefront of the IKV campaign against nuclear weapons and against the double-track decision. Besides this, we have always taken detente as an indivisible concept, in contrast to many political parties. For us, detente cannot only be reserved to the official policy or to commercial relations between East and West. No, detente should benefit the whole community. I will discuss later an important argument for this concept.

In Western Europe we are confronted with a very limited detente concept from the right wing. Commercial relations may increase, with a few exceptions (COCOM), but the military confrontation must continue and, last but not least, political confrontation must also continue. In order to accentuate the political confrontation, right wing groups try to monopolise the so-called dissidents in Eastern Europe. These brave people act as moral proof for their policy of military confrontation. Recent examples of this, taken from the Dutch situation, include a remark by our Prime Minister Ruud Lubbers that Charter 77 will not understand if the Netherlands refused to carry out the NATO double-track decision, and the distasteful manner in which the Russian dissident, Irnina Grevina, was recently welcomed at Schiphol Airport with a big show by the conservative VVD Party (liberal party). The Tamils from Sri Lanka, who fled to our country, are probably bewildered by the Dutch double standard in granting visas to refugees. Here a party of hardliners made bad political use of the very objectionable treatment that critics in Eastern Europe are subjected to. The social democratic concept of detente fortunately has a broader capacity, and political detente (*Entspannung von oben*) especially has been handled with strength and much "Erfolg". If the indications are reliable, military detente will come together with political detente; the often quoted and much applauded concept of common security (*Gemeinsame Sicherheit*) points in that direction.

Yet the Social Democrats have also put a limit to detente. Partly as a reaction to the abuse of the right wing, partly as a present to their political counterparts in Eastern Europe, they have decided practically to ignore critical voices in Eastern Europe, or at least not allow them a position in the great task of "Annaherung" between East and West. I am inclined to call this a fundamental mistake of the Social Democrats' detente policy, which at this point has been extended into a *system*. Ehmke makes this clear in his argument. He describes the political system in Eastern Europe as a system that exists for the benefit of the people but that makes its decisions without consulting their wishes. He argues that detente policy has contributed to this friction between the authorities and citizens in Eastern Europe becoming more bearable. People, however, do not want to be patronised. There is more room now. This, for example, is expressed in the fact that nowadays everyone in the GDR is able and allowed to receive West German television. In the Polish and Hungarian elections one can now choose from a double list of nominations — two nominees for one seat. There is more scientific, cultural, and economic exchange with the West and similar matters. But, as Ehmke seems to warn us, East European citizens have to be content with this for the present. The demand for political freedom and respect for individual human rights, which groups such as Charter 77 support, is unacceptable to Communist regimes. Ehmke regrets this, but he does not seem to come up with much beyond a resigned comment to the effect that, "You will have to learn to live with it." This is purely patronizing, and it will have a boomerang effect. Just consult any social psychologist and you will be told that as a citizen is offered more possibilities by the authorities, her or his demands will increase rather than decrease. Satisfaction will only occur when she or he can decide on her or his own life situation. In Eastern Europe they know this as well as we do. Ehmke seems to ignore this simple truth. He is liable to confused formulas such as: in moral respects they are right, Social Democrats should be aware of this, but political results are important and not the right disposition. Whereas, he once wrote that the internal dimension of detente in Europe, including relations with the dissidents, really has to be made "zum Gegenstand der Friedenspolitischen Erörterungen".

Detente from below is an addition to detente from above. It is no more and no less. One cannot exist without the other. They need one another. However, detente from below is more than merely the result of detente from above. It has its own dynamic. Politicians would do well to acknowledge this, and to respect this fact for what it is worth. It is easy to understand the fear which Ehmke and other Social Democrats share that detente from below and the independent operating of groups in the East as well as in the West will damage the political detente. But this thinking will have to be overcome. A constructive exchange and co-operation between below and above is a must.

As long as these two are seen as adversaries, then it will indeed turn into a self-fulfilling prophecy. The result will be that in Eastern as well as Western Europe there will be a certain state of mind which says that the Social Democrats give a slap on the back to those in power in Eastern Europe, but the man in the street doesn't really interest them. They ought to, or rather they must, be content with picking the fruits of detente from above. It is just this kind of arrogant use of power, "for you, but without you" which initiates protest from the peace movement. In Eastern Europe this is very clearly visible. Anyone who has walked around in Poland has discovered, with some dismay, the great sympathy which exists for the right wing in that country, because "they" (Reagan and his followers) do not treat the East European authorities with kid gloves. IKV is aware that as long as detente from below is not coupled with detente from above it runs the risk of being used by right wing politicians resulting in no detente whatsoever. Social Democrats, on the other hand, will also have to admit that for detente from above the days are numbered. People do not want to be merely the recipients of well-meant policies of others. They want to take part themselves. They want to take on the responsibilities for East-West relations in their own place in their society. This personal contribution is an essential aspect of what is called the *legitimation of power policies*. You cannot maintain a growing economy which is based on a shocking bureaucracy, no matter how beautiful the five or ten year plan might be. Space must be created for people to carry out their own initiatives. Of course, that should be within a certain framework, but still, it is only at that time that people will begin to trust such five year plans.

Fundamentally, it is no different in East-West detente. Citizens also demand the right to have their own ideas heard on the nuclear arms race, and to be able to search, together with their partners in other countries, for ways to stimulate the disarmament and detente process. The peace movement also claims this right, and therefore they make demands on the policies of left wing political parties, especially the Social Democrats' detente policy. Detente from below must take place within a political framework that spans East and West, and that can never be provided by the right wing. The politics of the right are based on confrontation and exclude Eastern Europe instead of including it. IKV wants political detente (downwards detente) in a second stage to provide very consciously the conditions under which contacts and relations between all sorts of institutions, groups, and persons from civil society can flourish more adequately and independently.

Ehmke shows to what degree a politician, a political party, or government in Western Europe as well as in Eastern Europe can be tempted to forget this independence, to dream that political power can legitimate itself and needs no "opponent", that it is always possible to manipulate civilians. He also tries to "buy" authority by means of propaganda and measures aimed at the public. This in itself is not even contestable, and corresponds with our opinion of democracy. Power must seek a legitimated status as a condition for democracy. And trust is therefore something like a medium of exchange that society grants to correct politics. For this reason, a politician will spend much time in recommending his goods. And that's the kind of thing Ehmke does. But in the end it will be a citizen's independent action to put trust in power (it is up to the customer!). And a citizen will do so if he or she is able to feel free (= responsible) under the power that is being exercised upon them. Everywhere this is the case, in both Western and Eastern Europe. In the case of a multi-party system, there are more possibilities to buy trust than in a one-party state. Moreover, it can be done crookedly.

A party, for instance the SPD in West Germany, can always refer to the bad policy, in their view, of the CDU/CSU, and consequently regard the loss of trust in the Christian Democrats as a gain for the Social Democrats. The former may be true; the second is a trick applied all too often in Western parliamentary democracies. In this respect, in communist states the Party is more vulnerable to the population. It tries to decrease its vulnerability by imposing several limitations on citizens, particularly in the realm of free expression of opinion. The often harsh measures against so-called dissidents are the excesses of this policy. However, even in a one-party state, the Party won't escape the necessity to legitimate its power. If it doesn't want to become a dictatorial state, this Party will have to leave its population space which is needed in order that it receive trust from that population. Anyone who follows the developments in Eastern Europe can see that governments there actually are conscious of this dilemma. This is not to deny that more room is developing in some East European countries. I'm referring particularly to Kadar's Hungary.

"Entspannung von oben", as any politics (von oben), pushes against limits in society. This could only change by giving room to that society to participate in its own way. The history of the *Bund der Evangelischer Kirchen in der DDR* is a good example. Ehmke understands this example, but in my opinion he restrains himself too much to an East European policy. This policy starts from the idea that one can grant nothing but that room to the people. In addition, for some reason(s), a very particular contribution has been excluded. One reason may be, for instance, the fear of losing power. But just for the sake of preserving power on a more democratic basis, in my opinion, it would be good to overcome this fear. *Entspannung von unten* has not necessarily destabilized the political system in Eastern Europe. On the contrary, why should Social Democrats not say this frankly to their partners in Eastern Europe?

Naturally, after the more fundamental remarks, the question arises: what good comes of all this in terms of practical politics? Firstly, a number of obstacles in the East-West relationship will have to be removed. One of these is the confrontation in Europe between the superpowers; I am in complete agreement with Ehmke on this. In this context I wish to remark that the European countries usually offer the superpowers all possible space to fight out their competition. The SPD cannot deny that their party has a major responsibility for the NATO double-track policy, and in my opinion it is not correct to make the United States answerable for all the misery this policy has brought. Nor is it correct to make answerable the other countries which had to join for the sake of the GDR.

In the light of detente, more thought must be given to other political and military relationships with the United States. The material performance of the alliance (NATO) must come under discussion. In this respect it concerns the extension of the American military, especially the nuclear presence in Europe. In this respect I should plead for making concrete the ideas of Von Bulow — *cum suis* — as well as about the measure of military integration. Von Bulow has gone in the wrong direction with regard to the latter point, from my point of view.

In fact he creates something like a West European army with a forward based concept in which the helicopter is introduced as a modern replacement for the tank. Regardless of the military objections to this alternative Maginot line, this approach affirms the division of Europe and forces the Soviet Union to maintain a military presence in Eastern Europe, and especially in the GDR. Still, I am not advocating that NATO and the Warsaw Pact be dismantled, but we must find a policy in which the symbols of bi-polar security, NATO and the Warsaw Pact, are gradually adapted to common security. For this it is especially important to convince the Soviet Union, just as it is the United States, of the necessity of pulling back their troops behind their own borders, with the exception of a symbolic few.

In my view, common security must be linked with the Helsinki process. The Conference on Security and Co-operation in Europe (CSCE) needs to gain more weight in Europe and should be institutionalised as soon as possible. This must happen quickly in order to prevent other new bi-polar forms of military integration such as the West European Union (WEU) and the IEPG, which may begin to dominate. Different elements of the detente process are brought together in the Helsinki Accords. This cohesion is important and should be understood as such and must be honoured. The third basket, humanitarian contacts, should no longer be viewed as a case apart whereby the parties can rebuke each other. This ideological decoupling of the third basket results in a decoupling of the other baskets as well. Sooner or later this will lead to stagnation at all levels.

In its recent policy programme (see footnote 3), IKV proposed that countries involved in the CSCE process should conclude bilateral Helsinki Accords. This counts for all countries in NATO and the Warsaw Pact. Helsinki is a landmark in the detente process, and should be built upon in the most creative way possible. To do this, IKV calls upon governments in East and West to develop a "contact policy" which would be geared specifically towards bringing their citizens together. In this way it is clear that more room can be created for individual initiatives from their respective citizens.

It would be too much to also set out here our ideas on EEC-Comecon relations, or to explain more generally how we feel about how economic and other contacts between East and West can be stimulated. In these areas too

68

we suggest a number of regulations which would give detente (a European
security interest) a more structural rather than a cyclical character
(dependent on fluctuations in the internal climate in the USA and the
USSR).

One last point. In all these years, IKV has seen that there is no area where
individual self-assurance is so absolute as peace and security. East and West
denounce each other. Governments and peace movements in Western
countries do very much the same. Dissidents in Eastern Europe are often
misused and maltreated. The social democratic parties rant and rave about
the peace movement and vice versa. Everyone seems to know what is best.
And this is done in the name of peace. Isn't it time that we learned to get
along with each other in a more creative fashion? If so, then we will have to
take the time and find the will to join in discussion with each other and learn
to listen to each other — preferably directly and not via distortions which are
made by a third party.

Footnotes

1. *Ton Veerkamp:* Gründsätzliche Gegensätze in der Friedensbewegung, Junge Kirche 3/85,
   S131FF. *Ton Veerkamp:* Blochfreies Europa — eine Perspective?, Die Neue Gesellschaft,
   Frankfurter Hefte IK, Nov. 1985, S1011FF.
2. *Horst Ehmke:* Frieden und Freiheit als Ziele des Entspannungspolitik, Die Neue
   Gesellschaft, Frankfurter Hefte II, Nov. 1985 S1003FF.
3. In IKV's 1970's detente policies, which are positively judged, there is a great deal of
   continuity. Look at the different papers which have been written. Compare especially the
   IKV paper "The future of Europe" with the chapter on East-West and detente in the IKV
   policy programme "peace politics" from 1985.
4. Strategie vertrauenschaffender Sicherheitsstructuren in Europa, Wege zur
   Sicherheitspartnerschaft. Entwurf einer Antrags zur Sicherheitspolitik für den
   Bundesparteitag 1986, Bonn, September 1985.

The Debate on Detente III: What kind of Detente?

IKV and SPD

An edited version of the discussion between the Interchurch Peace Council (IKV), Pax Christi The Netherlands, and the German Social Democratic Party (SPD), which took place on 12th March 1986 in Bonn. Peter Glotz is SPD General Secretary; Horst Ehmke is SPD Parliamentary Party Deputy Chairman; Karsten Voigt is a member of the SPD Disarmament Commission; Karl Heinz Koppe is an SPD Board member; Wolfgang Biermann is editor of the IFIAS Information Service; Mient Jan Faber, Laurens Hogebrink, and Wolfgang Müller are IKV representatives.

Peter Glotz asked the IKV to identify the faults in the SPD's detente policy.

Mient Jan Faber Fault is too harsh a term. We want to talk about broadening and including new elements in the existing detente policy. More contacts between the sections of civil society must be made possible, especially between groups and organisations in East and West. Detente policy should not only be defined from an economic and state-political point of view. Socio-political areas of detente politics are crucial for the peace movement. Detente from above and detente from below compliment each other.

Horst Ehmke described the problems the SPD has with human rights discussions related to Eastern Europe.
— The term 'human rights' is often used in a metaphorical way for democracy, which means that the desire to realise human rights is simultaneously an aspiration for the realisation of democracy.
— When dealing with human rights issues, the peace movement has to take care not to follow the spokesmanship of Dregger (Chairman of the CDU Parliamentary Party)
— The SPD believe that peace movements and political parties should have different positions in regard to the peace and human rights discusions. The peace movement and political parties have different tasks. The movements can allow themselves to be more radical.
— In terms of East-West politics the role of the SPD is very clear. Through detente policy it wishes to build up the basis for greater democracy in Eastern Europe without endangering detente policy itself.
— The human rights question primarily seems to be a humanitarian problem, but in reality it is an explosive political question which the SPD touches upon in its negotiations with the East European parties.
— The SPD sees no common ground with

'Radio Free Europe'. The radio station feeds the movement and the underground in Poland, which is also the opinion of the Polish Church.

— Poland provides an example of the breadth of the SPD's contacts. Contacts and exchanges take place with the party, the government, and the new trade union movement, as well as with the Catholic Church and Solidarnosc.

— The SPD does not favour only one organisation but wishes to have a broad dialogue. The implication is that in its discussions the SPD does not comment on the inner social processes. It wishes to avoid mediating between the groups and becoming involved in a conflict of interests. The SPD also wants to avoid that role so that if it assumes government it will not intervene as a state power in internal social developments which are the concern of a sovereign state.

Mient Jan Faber Participants in the END Convention (in Evry) will examine the continuation of detente politics. Why does the SPD show such little interest?

Horst Ehmke The SPD does not want to interfere in the peace movement's business nor influence it. There are a lot of voices advising against it. The peace movement should remain an independent force.

Wolfgang Biermann END is not representative of the West German peace movement because it consists only of fringe groups from the German peace movement. Another point is that the SPD did not take any position concerning Spanish membership of NATO while the END Convention spoke out against it.

Karl Heinz Koppe Only through detente can reform be achieved; detente itself can be endangered by contacts with the opposition. The SPD seeks the middle course. Unofficial contacts are maintained with reformers and dissidents. Official contacts only exist with official cadres. Thus the SPD has more difficulties with the German public; the press too readily believes the loud noises of the conservatives who vociferously support human rights in the East and indulge in public protest. The SPD path is pursued silently, without public relations exercises. It is successful and can moderate cases of hardship.

Peter Glotz When Willy Brandt visited Prague last year the SPD was faced with the question whether or not he should see Hajek. I was a member of the SPD delegation and I visited Charter 77 members such as Dienstbier, while through his official talks with President Husak, Willy Brandt managed to obtain commitments in five humanitarian cases. Charter 77 itself agreed with the SPD's strategy but regretted that Mr.Brandt could not visit them.

In this way through 'silent diplomacy' the SPD has been able to solve hardship cases in almost every East European country. This is much more important than the vocal propaganda heard from many groups which achieves nothing but creates the impression among the voters that the group is fighting for human rights.

Laurens Hogebrink How does one carry detente policy further? How does the SPD define the role of political groups inside the East-West relationship?

Karsten Voigt There should be a division of labour between party, state, and movement. This division of labour is only possible if the concept is not contradictory itself. The SPD has made mistakes through focusing only on state contacts with the East. As a party out of government it made almost no initiatives. The party should have its own independent task which also exists when we are in government. The East European parties, among others, work independently with their contacts in East and West even though they are permanently in government. Therefore, the SPD wants to redefine its role as a party in the East-West detente process. The division of labour should be:

— State level: to carry out negotiations with the character of binding international law, and to create new structures.

— Party politics level: to explain the fundamental guidelines of socialist politics; commitment to democracy and human rights must be clear; negotiations about that should not be carried out in public.

— Movement level: public action is fundamental, otherwise no treaties will be made. It has to be considered that some forms of action limit the political possibilities.

These three levels have to be separated clearly, and interactions taken into account.

Wolfgang Müller Mayors are seeking general framework agreements which would facilitate contacts on a basic level. If that is not possible on a multilateral scale then bilateral treaties should be concluded by the Helsinki signatories in East and West.

Horst Ehmke I don't believe in the 'feasibility' of bilateral agreements in different areas. The connection between the different elements of the Helsinki accords are not workable because the East will insist on two different treaties: a public one which would set regulations in the economic field favourable to the East; and a second one of an internal character containing regulations on human rights and humanitarian questions. The argument will be that humanitarian problems can be solved only through a private treaty, otherwise the Eastern country in question would have to show the treaty to its partner countries and explain it. It is not possible to pick out the question of democratisation in Eastern Europe as a central theme for bilateral talks.

Mient Jan Faber What do the SPD think about the negotiations in Geneva and the deployment decision, with the elections due in 1987?

Horst Ehmke There are people in the SPD who say that if the party comes to power in the elections then the deployment treaty with the Americans will be cancelled within six months and all Pershing II and cruise missiles withdrawn. I myself think that this is impossible. The 1985 party conference in Cologne set the goal which the SPD was to work for as the withdrawal of the American middle-range missiles and to ask the Soviet Union to withdraw the SS20s from the Western part of the Soviet Union as well as all SS22s and SS23s from East Germany and Czech territory.

The party conference due in August 1986 will be held with the elections in mind. At the conference both sides can be asked to withdraw their systems. The Cologne decision — 'we take away the American systems: the Soviet Union will be asked to withdraw theirs' — will not be repeated, in my opinion. It is not possible to get round the negotiations through unilateral withdrawal of US weapons while there exists the chance of an agreement in the Geneva negotiations. There is a danger that the SPD would find itself in a blind alley if the negotiations lead to a reduction of weapons.

As Richard Perle is making obvious efforts to bring the negotiations to a successful conclusion, this aspect may not be forgotten. As mentioned above, however, there are positions within the SPD which connect a clear 'no' to deployment with a unilateral withdrawal of all deployed systems.

Karsten Voigt explained the latest efforts of the SPD in the field of detente:

1. The arms race itself is defined as a source of tension and therefore undermines the pursuit of detente. The SPD recognises that detente has come to a stop especially because of the continuing escalation in armaments.

2. Concerning economic aspects of detente, politics should contribute to economic reform in the Soviet Union through increased East-West co-operation. At the moment the SPD is investigating what sort of co-operation, with which companies and sectors of the economy, can best serve to strengthen the reformists in the Soviet Union.

3. The content of detente is still under discussion in various talks with the communist parties. Important agreements have been reached with Czechoslovakia concerning protection of the environment. Talks with the Soviet Union concerning armaments and development aid are being held. Formerly, the Communist Party of the Soviet Union refused to discuss development questions with Western parties. Nowadays it is included in the dialogue. Talks with the GDR mainly concern security questions; a chemical weapon free zone in the FGR and the GDR has been agreed and other countries involved in Mutual Balanced Force Reductions (MBFR) may join. A remarkable aspect of this is the inclusion of the right of each signatory country to monitor adherence to the treaty throughout the whole area covered. It is also important to be aware of the fact that several East European communist parties have begun to define their own interests because of these talks. A happy consequence has been that this did not always take place in co-ordination with the Warsaw Pact's common interest. This is one of the reasons why the Soviet Union does not always support these talks. Formerly, the Soviet Union was more enthusiastic about them

because they were taking place in the spirit of the "new alliance" with progressive forces in the West. However, since they have led to increased independence of the Soviet Union on the part of the East European states, the Soviet Government wishes to oppose this development. They hold these talks consciously within the framework of the Conference on Security and Co-operation in Europe. The party would like other West European countries to participate in this dialogue, especially the Benelux ones. We need not anticipate the development of German bilateralism. The SPD simply took the initiative — other countries should follow.

Why Sanctions Are Imperative

*Archbishop
Desmond Tutu*

*This is the text of a
statement made by the
Archbishop in
Johannesburg on 2 April
1986.*

In 1976, out of a growing and deepening apprehension about the mood in Soweto, one of increasing anger, bitterness, and frustration, I wrote an open letter to the then Prime Minister, Mr. B.J. Vorster. In it, I was warning him that unless something was done and done urgently to remove the causes of black anger, I was fearful of what was likely to erupt because black people were growing increasingly restive under the oppressive yoke of *apartheid* and, for young people, it was represented in the insensitive determination to enforce on them Afrikaans as a medium of instruction in their inferior schools in a system of education that had been designed for inferiority by its author, Dr. Verwoerd. My letter was dismissed contemptuously by Mr. Vorster as a propaganda ploy somehow engineered by the Progressive Federal Party. He did not even think that I, as a black person, could have the intelligence to know the grievances of my own people, or the ability if I did to compose a letter to express those grievances.

A few weeks later, on 16th June, the Soweto uprising happened, and since then South Africa has had no real peace or stability.

I refer to this first effort to show that, for over 10 years, I have attempted to alert authorities in this land to the dangers to which their misguided and iniquitous policies were exposing our beloved country. In that 1976 letter I had referred to some of the minimum conditions that would enable blacks to feel that their plight was being taken seriously. I have made many public statements urging the Government to act decisively and to give blacks hope.

On many occasions since then, I have intervened in delicate and volatile situations to try and help defuse them. I have gone with other black and white leaders to Turfloop and Fort Hare Universities to offer our good offices to resolve the perennial problems relating to student boycotts on those campuses. This was the action of some one who believes that problems can be solved by people sitting down together to discuss their differences. This has been a fundamental stance on my part. I have spoken to various white groups and addressed audiences at all the white university campuses (except the University of Port Elizabeth). I have even been to the University of the Orange Free State and I can tell you that that was something else. I have been to some of these universities often more than just once. I was criticized by the black community for doing so, because it was said that I was just wasting time. I believed and I still believe that we must try to undo the evil consequences of *apartheid*. One of these is that white and black don't really know one another, and so I was ready, as I still am, to talk especially to young whites to help them see and think in the hope that, by thinking independently, they would come to reject this horrendous policy, which is so utterly evil, immoral, and unchristian, and which their fathers and mothers have tended to support, and, by their rejection, to help save our country from catastrophe, for I still believe in young people. Black and white will be our salvation.

Negative Responses from Government

In 1980, on my initiative, some of the leaders of the South African Council of Churches (SACC), and of member churches, went to see Mr. P.W.Botha, who was then Prime Minister, and his senior cabinet colleagues. We were trying to make them understand that unrest would be endemic in South Africa unless its root cause was removed — and that root cause was *apartheid*.

We declared then that we knew that politics was the art of the possible and did not want to suggest they do anything that would erode their support among their constituencies. We put forward four things which, if done, would be a dramatic demonstration of the Government's intention to effect real political change leading to political power sharing. Remember this was in 1980, six years ago. We said that the Government should:

(a) Declare a commitment to a common citizenship for all South Africans in an undivided South Africa;

(b) Abolish the pass laws (even a phased abolition to avoid chaos), detention without trial, and arbitrary banning;

(c) Stop all forced population removals immediately;

(d) Establish a uniform education system.

These were not wild, radical demands, and if the Government had implemented them then, we would have been saved a great deal of anguish, bloodshed, loss of property, and an increase in bitterness, hatred, and anger. We were criticized by the black community for going to the Government. These were much of the same conditions presented in my 1976 letter to Mr. Vorster. But do you know what happened? They were ignored. In fact, we later discovered that the Government had dealt dishonourably with us. While we were discussing with them in good faith, all the while they were employing the Christian League as a front organisation in their nefarious efforts to subvert, malign, and discredit SACC, as was to be revealed in the infamous information scandal. Actually, the Government intensified its efforts to undermine the Council and me personally by getting its sycophantic South African Broadcasting Corporation (SABC), and other of its lickspittle media supporters to denigrate and vilify us, culminating in the Eloff Commission to investigate SACC. That ended with the Government being embarrassed with a lot of egg on its face. SACC and I received a global vindication by the award of the Nobel Peace Prize. The Government was thoroughly hoist with its own petard because our member churches and overseas supporters rallied to our support in an unprecedented way.

Despite all this negative response from the Government, I was often in delegations to see various government ministers, trying to make them take different attitudes, especially on the issues of forced population removal and education. Mr. Barend Du Plessis, then Minister for Black Education, publicly thanked me for helping to defuse the situation in Atteridgeville before the funeral of the Sathege girl who had been run over by a police car. He has thus far been the only Government minister to my knowledge to have done so. We had gone to Atteridgeville with the Reverend S.Mogoba on behalf of SACC. I was just carrying out my belief that we must try to talk ourselves out of a crisis. I offered myself as a go-between for the Government and the African National Congress of South Africa, long before it was fashionable to go to Lusaka, in the hope that the authorities would seize an opportunity to start the negotiations that are inevitable if we are to save our country from disaster.

In 1984, far from heeding our calls for negotiation leading to power sharing, the Government introduced a constitution that was the climax of the policies of exclusion to which blacks had been subjected since 1910. Seventy three per cent of the population was excluded from any participation in this monumental hoax designed to hoodwink the international community that *apartheid* was being reformed.

Apartheid Must Be Destroyed

Apartheid is irreformable. It must be destroyed before it destroys our country. That constitution was meant to entrench white minority rule with the co-opted help of so-called Coloureds and Indians, collaborators in their own, and our, oppression and exploitation. The people have rejected it unequivocally, and August 1984 saw the beginning of the current wave of unrest.

Despite all this, I tried again last year to see the State President to talk with him as one South African to a fellow South African, as one grandfather to another, as one Christian to another, in the hope that he would act as only he could, the one white South African for whom blacks would have been ready to erect a statue as the man who would have gone down in history as presiding over the dissolution of *apartheid* and the emergence of a new, more equitable, just, non-racial, and truly democratic South Africa. He turned me down. In parenthesis, I might add that I said he needed to be commended for his courage in telling whites that there was no way in which they alone could determine the future of this country forever. Sadly, he did not go far enough, and so ended up pleasing neither the blacks nor his so-called right wing. To turn an English expression around, we see the sad spectacle of a man who does not have the convictions of his courage. Yet, I was ready to go to Alexandra Township to help defuse the tense situation there and to go in a delegation to Cape Town to talk with the Government about that situation and the situation in the country. Nothing in South Africa, or very little, has changed without pressure from the international communities. The sports policy changed only as a result of the sports boycott, which I have supported and will continue to do so as a non-violent method to bring about change. I have called upon the international community to exert on the Government political, diplomatic, but above all, economic pressure to persuade it to go to the negotiating table with the authentic representatives of all sections of our society, and I have said, for blacks, that this would mean those in gaol or in exile. I have said this umpteen times. I have been accused of advocating sanctions and I have said that I have not yet called for sanctions. I have said that each country should surely decide for itself the nature of the economic pressure it wishes to apply.

I have lost my passport on a few occasions, once for two weeks because I was accused of advocating sanctions. I have been consistently attacked in the media as such an advocate. South Africans are so good at finding scapegoats and enemies, instead of dealing with the problem that stares us in the face. The scapegoat at one time was the total onslaught. But you can't have a total onslaught if you have signed accords, and so you look for other "enemies" as the red herrings to avoid dealing with the real issues. I have been depicted by nearly all the white media, even the so-called responsible, liberal English newspapers, as that "public enemy". They have succeeded in inciting whites to a pitch of hostility where they must take the responsibility if whites do then kill such as ourselves. That is particularly true of SABC — they are guilty of incitement to violence. That is another matter and we will deal with it yet. Most western countries have rejected economic sanctions because we are told that they would hurt blacks most of all. I hope that those who use this argument will just drop it quietly and stop being so hypocritical. It is amazing how everybody has become so solicitous for blacks and become such wonderful altruists. It is remarkable that in South Africa the most vehement in their concern for blacks have been whites. Very few blacks have repudiated me for my stance. This is very odd. They are not stupid. If they knew they were going to suffer, then they would reject out of hand one who wanted to bring that suffering on them. Yet, in the black community, my standing is very high. Even more remarkably, two recent surveys have shown that over 70 per cent of blacks supported sanctions of some sort. Blacks have carried out consumer boycotts. They have staged massive stay-aways to make a political statement.

Punitive Sanctions: A Non-violent Response to Government Violence
Over 1,200 blacks have died since August 1984. Blacks are killed mainly by the security forces, almost as if they were flies. Children are detained. Children are killed. It is alleged that 50 were shot in the back outside a court.

I have heard hardly a squeak from the whites who claim they are concerned for black suffering. They say the state of emergency has been lifted. On Easter Sunday, I saw a Casspir rumbling down Soweto highway. On Easter Monday, in our part of Soweto, much the most quiet part, four Casspirs and personnel carriers drove past my house. My wife said, "the border is here". The troops are still in the township since the Durban Education Conference, which took a brave decision about the children staying in school, and we have the insensitivity of the authorities displaying their military might when they know the presence of troops in the townships is highly provocative.

Nothing that Mr. Botha has said has made me believe that he and his Government are serious about dismantling *apartheid*. He says we are one nation and, just as we are rejoicing, then he says we are a nation of minorities — unadulterated and dangerous nonsense of bantustans. If we are one nation, then why should Kwandebele be going for this spurious independence? Why should the people of Moutse die to satisfy a racist ideology?

We hear that there will be an end to the pass laws and we say "Hurray", and then we hear that there will be some "orderly urbanization". Since orderly urbanization will apply to them alone, some of the influx control will have to be applied.

But the giveaway is surely the public dressing down that Mr. Pik Botha got. For once, when he was speaking the truth, he was repudiated. He was not so repudiated when he lied about the South African troops in Angola, or about aiding the *Movimiento Nacionalista Revolucionerio (MNR)*. The State President said there would be power sharing. Surely the sheer arithmetic of South Africa should indicate that there will be a black President. Even the law of averages decrees this if we have one nation. The State President supported the most reactionary of his ministers with regard to the Group Areas Act, which relies on the equally obnoxious Population Registration Act.

And then there were the devastating resignations of Dr. Van Zyl Slabbert and Dr. Borraine The media played down their significance. These two gentlemen were endorsing our long-stated views that parliament in South Africa is a mere charade. The Progressive Federal Party has always given the world the illusory impression that we have parliamentary democracy, when we really have a one-party State that is viciously oppressive and unjust and violent in putting down opposition and dissent. You are banned, detained, or charged with high treason. I have no hope of real change from the Government unless they are forced. We face a catastrophe in this land, and only the action of the international community, by applying pressure, can save us. Our children are dying. Our land is burning and bleeding, and so *I call upon the international community to apply punitive sanctions against this Government* to help us establish a new South Africa that is non-racial, democratic, participatory, and just. This is a non-violent strategy to help us to do so. There is a great deal of goodwill still in our country between the races. Let us not be so wanton in destroying it. We can live together as one people, one family, black and white together.

Reviews

History, Reason and Joy

Society and Puritanism in Pre-revolutionary England, by Christopher Hill, Peregrine Books, 1986, £5.95
Puritanism and Revolution, by Christopher Hill, Peregrine Books, 1986, £4.95
Capitalism and Social Democracy, by Adam Przeworski, Cambridge University Press, 1985, £25

Serendipity — a happy accident. These books of two totally different kinds turned up for review at the same time. And the coincidence made me wonder what political theory has to do with what actually happens in history.

Przeworski analyses doctrines that have guided socialist movements over, roughly, the last century and a half. His book is excellently written and embodies a wealth of intelligent thought and textual research. Christopher Hill's books are republications, with some corrections but no major alterations, of work done more than thirty years ago. They are 'modern classics' for the history of our 17th Century Revolution. The great beauty of the Hill books is the authentic awareness of the times that they pass on to the reader. This awareness lives in the incidents, the words spoken or written and the people he calls in evidence. What emerges is a simple but momentous fact: a profound social revolution was under way in 16th and 17th century Britain. And it is the genius of these books that they pass on to us a living sense of what a social revolution is like. This for our present times is a matter of no small importance because — as I see it — the world is once again engaged in a social revolution, not now just for one or a few nations but for all humankind, the social revolution that is asserting democracy, people-power, classlessness and equality of rights for all against elitism, hierarchy and privilege. To navigate these stormy seas of social change we need to sense its complexities and many-sidedness.

But how did 17th Century history on the one hand and, on the other, political theories of socialism connect in my mind? In fact they connected fiercely as I shuddered to think how many hours of my life — and of many others — had gone in reading, arguing, thinking about "roads to socialism". Then I see the fluttering words of these heated theorisings neatly netted in Adam Przeworski's book and "formulated, sprawling on a pin". What, I wonder, is the connection between all this and the turmoil of historical change that will in fact come about?

In the 16th and 17th centuries the framework of argument was religious doctrine. Today the doctrinal disputes are about political theory. In crudest outline the argument which Przeworski records is whether socialists should concentrate on the winning of state power and only then begin the building of a new socialist world *or* build socialism bit by bit into existing society until the totality of the new bits finally adds up to a new society. He explores this old argument between "revolutionary socialism" and "reformism" with care and accuracy and, finding both positions flawed, opts for neither one of them. For him, as for many of us, the idea of socialism, ill-defined as it may be, still points the direction to be taken. After dismantling what have hitherto been the main established socialist doctrines, Przeworski only very briefly hints at his own alternative (pp.247-8):

> "The need for freedom is integral. Socialist democracy is not something to be found in parliaments, factories or families; it is not simply a democratisation of capitalist institutions. Freedom means de-institutionalisation; it means individual autonomy. Socialism may perhaps become possible, but only on the condition that the movement for socialism regains

the integral scope that characterised several of its currents outside the dogmas of the Internationals, only on the condition that this movement ceases to make the socialist project conditional upon the continual improvement of the material conditions of the working class. It may become possible when socialism once again becomes a social movement and not solely an economic one, when it learns from the women's movement, when it reassimilates cultural issues."

There are phrases in this statement that I would argue with but its main thrust is, I am sure, right. In social revolution all aspects of human existence are at issue: the theories abstract only aspects of the whole. This contrast, between the thin schematism of doctrine and theory and the wayward complexity of the historical events that they hoped to influence, struck me forcibly when I had these different books together in my hand.

More and better socialist theory is badly needed. The need is for democratic theory, that is theory closely attuned to the needs and experiences of people themselves. A socialist economy requires control over resources by people themselves in contrast to control by the automaticity of money-power or control *for* people by bureaucratic power. But theory itself can become an instrument of power over people and so democratic politics needs to have a bit more theory about the dangers of theory. We need a style that is much more temperate, much less dogmatic and simplistic in the use of such insights as theory may give.

Socialist culture must embrace moral and political pluralism and avoid the fanatical excesses which championed or opposed the early capitalism of which Christopher Hill writes. Yet democracy requires vigour and dedication against the barbarities with which elitists too often defend their interests. However, the vigour of dogmatism and fanaticism negates democracy by cancelling the right of free people to think and act for themselves.So the vigour of democracy has to be rooted in love of freedom, in the joy that freedom gives. Joy itself is an expression of specific cultures. The joy of those who take joy in oppressing others can be no part of a socialist culture; the joy we must have is joy that springs from the fulness of life. Social revolution today is about the flowering of a many-sided culture of freedom to which political theory is no more than instrumental. Instruments we need, but they should not be allowed pretensions above their status. So political theory should be modest about its limitations. Christopher Hill's writing about the 17th Century helps one greatly to get a proper sense of proportion; the political theory of those times, particularly that which was clothed in religious language, was a significant agent of change but, at the level of consciousness, social revolution was very much more than that; it was a far reaching cultural transformation. And it is not only from books that human beings learn; writing during the Second World War, Pearl Buck said (Foreword to essays on "Asia and Democracy", 1943):

"There are certain trends of common thought . . . [which] . . . proceed, in waves and jerks and shocks of comprehension . . . . People all over the world have not only been fighting a war — they have also been undergoing a violent education."

Still — nearly half a century later on — this process continues as people of all parts of the world learn common interests and awaken to the potential power of the democratic vision. But one lesson is still very hard to learn, that is, how to show tolerance of different views and different modes of struggle against oppression without making this an excuse for abandoning struggle. Such tolerance without self-deception is of the essence of the democratic culture that has still to be learned.

Stephen Bodington

"Keep Them Confused"*
Clouds of Deceit: The Deadly Legacy of Britain's Bomb Tests, by Joan Smith, London, Faber, 1985, 176pp., £4.95

Following the Chernobyl disaster Western spokesmen and media were faced with a distressing situation: here was a golden opportunity for venting anti-Soviet sentiments which they, nevertheless, could not manipulate as much as they would have wished. Unfortunately, the general public was awakening to the dangers of nuclear power and was unlikely to be convinced that capitalist radiation was harmless if communist radiation endangered the world. Unable to let such a propaganda coup slip through their fingers, the opinion formers settled on Soviet secrecy as the key danger in the whole situation: the Russians preferred to sacrifice their own and other people rather than openly provide the information necessary to deal with the accident. However much truth is in that opinion, it came strangely from countries such as Britain with its record of secrecy after the Windscale accident. The West needs few lessons in suppression of information — or in disregard of the impact on its citizens of scientific (or industrial) practices.

In the light of this, Joan Smith's account of the British nuclear tests in the 1950s, the secrecy and lies which surrounded them, the cavalier attitude towards the impact of radiation on both service personnel and the Australian aborigines, and the connivance of the media in backing up the whole macabre charade, comes most opportunely. It is a story which, even 30 years later, could not have been pieced together without the information extracted by the Australian Royal Commission; it is also a story which her employers at the *Sunday Times* did their best to suppress. (This latter aspect is recounted in her introduction and should be noted by anyone who still has illusions about the "quality" newspapers in Britain.)

Robert Jungk argued years ago that the nuclear state would necessarily lead to the totalitarian state. The need to suppress information and deal with the dissenters is by now evident: Karen Silkwood, probably Hilda Murrell, are victims of the nuclear industry just like the Marshallese. And the attempted suppression and denigration of the work of Alice Stewart and Thomas Mancuso on the effects of low-level radiation is one of many examples of distortions and fears by which the nuclear establishment hopes to defuse opposition to its insane policies. Those opposing are either scientifically wrong or, the smears imply, agents of foreign interests — traitors. In this context, Smith recalls Joseph Rotblat's shock when, in 1944, at a time when Russia was our ally and taking the savage brunt of German attacks, the US general in charge of the Manhattan project calmly observed to the scientists co-operating to produce the atomic bomb: "You realize that all our work is against the Russians?" But for the mass media the traitors have always been those who could not rejoice in the achievement which restored Britain's war-ravaged confidence. Smith's accounts of the media's love affair with the bomb in the 1950s — including that of Chapman Pincher BSc — are timely reminders that the propaganda surrounding the nuclear issue was an inherent part of its development from the moment the USA and its junior partner realized its political potential. This disinformation campaign was carried out at every level from Sir William Penney, in charge of the tests, and Lord Cherwell, Churchill's scientific advisor, down through the years to Margaret Thatcher or Ministry of Defence spokesmen like Adam Butler or Geoffrey Pattie who are still telling us that all is well; "safety precautions were taken that compare favourably with the international standards in force today", Pattie told MPs in 1984, which may be true but is hardly comforting. People who

*President Eisenhower on what to tell the public about the hydrogen bomb, 1953.

expressed doubts were vilified, like Linus Pauling, or, in the case of the distinguished Australian scientist, Sir Mark Oliphant, kept away from the tests because the *Americans* considered him a security risk.

Two examples of the deception she recounts: it was not until 1984 that the British government admitted that the second atomic test in Monte Bello in 1956 was three times bigger than previously stated (60, not 20 kilotons); such frankness was somewhat diminished when "secret documents released to the Public Records Office in 1985 suggested it was even bigger than the 1984 descriptions — 98 kilotons." British deception towards the Australian government (and people) whose soil they were using was as bad: "the true size of the biggest bomb, the 98 kiloton Mosaic II blast — nearly eight times as large as the Hiroshima bomb — was concealed from the Australian government for 29 years.

For many of the thousands of British servicemen who attended the tests the results have been, and continue to be, devastating. Cancer, sterility, and lesser problems have dogged many of them who are now, belatedly, fighting for compensation. Their bitterness and feelings of betrayal are illustrated by the RAF squadron leader, dying from a radiation induced cancer, who, in 1983, phoned the chairman of the British Nuclear Tests Veterans Association to say: "I'm phoning on behalf of my widow. When I die, I want you to get those bastards." A month later he was dead. The servicemen were told almost nothing about what they were doing, were provided with the most casual of radiation protection or monitoring, and were leaned on very heavily to keep their mouths shut.

Following the discovery of an aborigine family camping in one of the bomb craters at Maralinga in 1957, the troops were "lined up and warned that they would be court-martialled if they spoke about the family to anyone outside the test site. They were told the penalty they would get if found guilty was either death or 30 years in prison." The area was considered "unpopulated" — the aborigines did not count. (One can see President Botha smiling, thinly.)

But this is not simply an account of the deceits of 30 years ago. It is very much an on-going story, for it seems likely that the 1950s servicemen got radiation doses "smaller than those received routinely every year by workers in the nuclear industry." And, as Smith observes, "if men exposed to such tiny doses of radiation have suffered elevated rates of disease, what future is there for the nuclear industry, which exposes its workers annually to more radiation than most veterans received once in their lifetime?" Not that 1950s exposures were limited to test veterans and victims. In 1958 John Dunster, then of the UKAEA (and now director of the National Radiological Protection Board, which gives pause for thought) told a UN conference that discharges from Windscale were "part of a deliberate experiment to find out more about the movement of radioactive substances in the environment". These discharges are now suspected of causing the high levels of leukemia near the plant. Perhaps the North Wales farmers who suspected the reactors at Trawsfynydd and Wlyfa rather than Chernobyl when the government banned slaughter because of radiation levels in the sheep were not so far off the mark.

The result of America's determination to exploit its position of superiority after getting the atomic bomb is the distrust which fuels the arms race. The slowly emerging result of the radiation impact of those early tests is "a time-bomb under every nuclear power station in Britain." Joan Smith has done us a major service in helping expose and publicise the issues involved.

Anne Buchanan

Cops and Robbers in New Zealand

Death of the Rainbow Warrior, by Michael King, London, Penguin Books, 254 pp.

This is a curious book — and an unsatisfying one, in spite of the author's modest claim that "it comes as close as any book can to being the full story of what happened in New Zealand in the course of Operation Rainbow Warrior". It is a tribute to the author's singlemindedness that it was completed in spite of "apparent attempts at seduction, industrial sabotage, French surveillance of my own activities and competition for film rights" during the period of writing (author's prefatory note).

It is curious because the lengthy and verbatim police interrogations of the two agents who *were* captured — Prieur and Mafart — which form a key part of the book, and which are supplemented by graphic accounts of the behaviour of both interrogator and accused (e.g. p.179), were not supplied by the police but came from sources the author is unable to divulge (p.253). The line to be drawn between protecting confidentiality of sources and the use, as by governments, of the plea that security would be endangered, were the source of their otherwise unsupported assertions to be disclosed, is a broad and hazy one. But in the case of this volume, the author's reticence makes an adequate review virtually impossible.

It's a disappointing book on several counts. First, because (in spite of a nod in the direction of the Marshall Islands in chapter 1), there is little attempt to put the Rainbow Warrior episode into perspective as part of an obscene — and insane — competition between France and the United States and Britain to gain some sort of lead in the race towards mutual extinction, a competition whose costs are borne by the Australian aboriginals and the indigenous people of the Pacific. Secondly, it is disappointing as an essay in investigative journalism because treatment of the relations between the NZ Security Intelligence Service (SIS) and the NZ Police is perfunctory; for example, there is no discussion of the claims in the local press that the SIS valued its cosy relationship with its French counterpart (DGSE) more than with the NZ police, resulting in delays in releasing information to the latter. The "security community" transcends national frontiers and indeed it is claimed in New Zealand that the SIS had a DGSE liaison officer. Thirdly, the book is disappointing in that it does not explain satisfactorily just why the NZSIS should have failed to detect the presence at various times in the country of half a score of French agents who scarcely troubled to keep a low profile. Dr King categorically states that the SIS, "had no prior intelligence about the presence or movements of French agents in New Zealand" (p.170). Why not? Fourthly, the book is disappointing because of the deadening accumulation of trivia: what Mafart wore during his interrogation; the detailed menu of Mafart and Prieur at Papillon, one of Auckland's better French-style restaurants (p.165); Mafart's prison diet, "roast beef or chicken..." (pp.208-9); the unremitting energy of one agent (one of the many who escaped) who seduced eight different women in seven days (p.115); the details of various agents cavorting in up-country "night spots"...all these things convey the impression of a desperate attempt to generate "wordage".

King's conclusions were overtaken by events. The angry denials by the NZ government that some sort of "lamb-chop spy deal" was being arranged, as was alleged in some European newspapers (p.221); David Lange's assertion that neither the agents "nor the New Zealand judicial system were up for sale" (p.228), ring hollow after the Perez de Cuellar judgement (which was delivered before the book was published). According to this judgement, France was to pay $13 million in compensation and give assurances it would cease opposing New Zealand's attempts to build up an export market for dairy produce and meat within the EEC. For its

84

part, New Zealand abandoned its emphasis on full implementation of the sentence of 10 years imprisonment imposed on the two agents. New Zealand's submission to the UN Secretary-General emphasised that "it has been, and remains, essential to the NZ position that there should be no release to freedom, that any transfer should be to custody, and that there should be a means of verifying that." Perez de Cuellar's arbitration ignored this: the prisoners were to be transferred for three years to the French Pacific military base at Hao and will be able to mix with their family and friends and with military personnel. There is no mention of any action against other French agents who had converged on New Zealand for the terror attack on the Rainbow Warrior, including those who planted the bombs.

The lesson is clear: only a country with a high degree of self-sufficiency in its economy can hope to adopt and maintain a moral stance in the jungle to which the great powers have reduced international order. The further down the road a country is to the "Society of Consumption", the more vulnerable it becomes; the moral collapse of the NZ government's original position in this affair has its roots in the type of society to which the government's economic planners are committed.

Meanwhile, France is rocked by a spate of bombings and Jacques Chirac has declared "when those responsible...are caught, they will be punished without mercy" (19th September 1986), and in Indonesia Mitterrand himself emphasised that "terrorism must be fought without mercy" (17th September). Given that recent French reports suggest that, notwithstanding the clouds of disinformation and lies which have surrounded *l'affaire Greenpeace*, Mitterrand himself may have been privy to this act of state terrorism, these declarations add the final sordid, hypocritical touch to another despicable manifestation of "Great Power" arrogance in international affairs.

Keith Buchanan

Green Fundamentals

Building the Green Movement, by Rudolf Bahro, London, GMP Publishers, 1986.

Rudolf Bahro is a prophet for our times. His insights are penetrating and many-sided. He sharpens the sensibilities of all who are concerned for the human predicament. Socialists and democrats should listen carefully to what he has to say in this book. He sees one single system — what he calls the Big Machine — taking over and corrupting all aspects of human existence; and, describing himself as a fundamentalist, he urges us to break with this system root and branch.

With Rudolf Bahro's concept of the Big Machine I, broadly speaking, go along; and so I am often excited by the sharpness with which, using this general framework, he brings particular issues into focus. For me the "Big Machine" is the automatic workings of commodity relations and the swift autocracy of money-power that this enthrones. Moreover it is certainly true that this order of things pervades more and more aspects of world-wide human existence. Further, what once was a liberating solvent breaking the autocracy and obscurantism of feudal and absolutist social orders has grown into a monster which the more it grows the more it corrupts and brings closer threats of annihilatory destruction. Where I part company with Rudolf Bahro is when he starts to preach his "fundamentalism". Statements such as "The only work which will stop the apocalypse is to cleanse and assemble the psychological forces for an Ecopax formation of biophile culture" (p.176) seem to me more like hallucinatory drugs than food that builds muscles for struggle.

My feelings, reinforced by rational analysis, urge me to believe that it is the struggle of the many to take over social power from the few that alone can save the human species. This struggle is revolutionary in the sense that it strives to make new social values prevail and to establish a new structure of social relations capable of controlling and subordinating money-power. But this does not mean all or nothing change from the world as it now is. Rather it means finding footholds in this world from which to struggle for change. Where these footholds are and how they can best be used, freedom and justice loving people have to discover in their own ways.

Criticism of such empty phrases as "we cannot afford any more reformist half-measures" (p.176) should not be taken to imply objection to what in Bahro is almost a religious approach to politics. It is in my view a serious defect of democratic and socialist movements that they have failed to guide and help their members in all aspects of living, spiritual, cultural, and material. What religion has done for people in societies of old, 'congregations' or 'orders' of socialists and democrats could far more powerfully do today to strengthen dedication and give social impact to the truth of new human values. Bahro's originality of approach to our gropings in this direction — and they still are only gropings — should be carefully attended to. We cannot look to him for solutions but there is much to learn from the general direction of his thinking on these matters.

The framework of ideas through which Bahro sees the place of human beings in relation to the environment of nature is very powerful and the sharpened perceptions that this gives can easily be separated off from his tendency to over-certainty and fundamentalism. That is, don't let the high seriousness of his style cause a switch off of critical faculties. For example, however right his decision to leave the Green Party may or may not be, the reason he gives for it is not a good one. He feels he must dissociate himself from an organisation that accepts experiments on animals given specified controls. So to do he says (p.210) "expresses the basic principle by which human beings are exterminating plants, animals and finally themselves." On such a difficult question — are not all living creatures living in some degree at the expense of others? — can individual A, say, break with B, C and D because their formulations do not coincide with his? If B, C and D are honest persons and not tricksters, A has a duty to attend to their views and where they can't agree to compromise. Of course, there may be dirty compromises hiding conspiracy to betray causes, but compromise is also a *sine qua non* of collaboration between honest people. My quarrel with fundamentalist dedication to principle is that true principle lives in the world of contradictory realities where keeping faith with human values calls for accurate judgement of changing circumstances. Too much fervour for principle in general and too little attention to the witness of others about particular circumstances can surrender living truth to dead dogma.

Most of the points on which I do not go along with Rudolf Bahro relate back, I believe, to what one might call "the democratic dimension". Many socialists and democrats take too little account of the implications of democratic practice. They work out policies, theories and principles without taking account of this dimension, as if it could be added on without affecting the soundness of views arrived at independently of democratic practice. How can this be if, as I think is right, no principle is set higher than that of enabling people generally to control for themselves the collective activities of which they are part? In the last analysis people learn most by doing; hence the importance of creating opportunities for people to control what they do and how they do it. Bahro's criticism of Mike Cooley suggests confusion on this point. "What I still criticise in Mike Cooley" he says (p.122) is "that he always starts from the assumption that the worker must remain a worker and the engineer an engineer, and that we just have to convert to more acceptable products. That is not radical enough for me . . . " I don't suppose Mike Cooley assumes anything of the sort — but that is not the point. The point is, starting from the situations in which people find themselves, to enable people to grasp and hence determine the social meaning of their own activities. The Lucas Aerospace Shop Stewards' Committee started asking simple questions about redundancy and advanced to a collective consciousness of how criteria of social usefulness should override criteria of exchange-value. It was democratic activity in practice. Such activity in community life as well as in existing work units would lead far away from existing technologies and divisions of labour. The radical thing is not only to be socially long-sighted, as Bahro undoubtedly is, but to struggle for conditions in which people generally can make their futures for themselves. People so liberated are the only lasting bulwarks against species-suicide.

John Eaton

Marx-and-Engels De-linked

Marx and Engels: The Intellectual Relationship by Terrell Carver. Brighton, Wheatsheaf, 1983, 172pp, £25.

A Japanese friend once told me that it is not uncommon for young Japanese Marxists, who may be unfamiliar with European languages, to believe that 'Marx-and-Engels' was a single person. The joke, however, may be on those of us in the West who have accepted the view that Marx and Engels had a close co-operative intellectual relationship, and that they were in mutual, strong agreement about their independent as well as their joint works. If this view were correct, 'Marx-and-Engels' might just as well have been one person as two independently creative minds.

In his excellent study of the intellectual relationship between the two founders of Marxism, Terrell Carver shows that there is more mythology than substance in the prominent view that Marx and Engels were close, or even interchangeable, collaborators in thought. The orthodox account of a close and common outlook was presented by Engels, and only in the later years of Marx's life and after his death. Just as Marxism became popularised through the version presented of it by Engels in his book *Anti-Duhring* (this sold far more copies than *Capital* in the decades when Marxism was first gaining popularity), the accepted view of the intellectual relationship between the two founders became that of Engels rather than Marx.

By careful argument and textual study, Carver presents a complex and different view. Given that the convention has been to rely on Engels' account of the intellectual relationships, he concentrates on a close portrait of Engels' intellectual development, from the time before he met Marx. Several conclusions follow from this study. For example, he shows that parts of *Communist Manifesto* (published of course in their joint names) are attributable to an earlier work by Engels. Thus Engels was responsible for much of the emphasis on class struggle and the historical material, and Marx more for the political economy.

Another topic is 'dialectics'. Carver shows that Engels is responsible for the commonplace presentation of Marx as the successor of Hegel. In fact the concern with and reaction to Hegel was more from Engels than Marx, and started with his political controversy with the Young Hegelians. As always, even in his early works, Marx was more concerned with the development of his critique of political economy. Consequently, Marx cannot be understood without understanding him as an economist, and we get a distorted view by approaching him mainly as a post-Hegelian philosopher.

The claim that their work was 'materialist' first appears in a published work by Engels as late as 1859. Engels too is responsible for the idea that 'scientific socialism' is built on a universal method, which applies to natural as well as social science. Engels described this philosophy as 'dialectical' and 'materialist', and Marxist successors later invented the phrase 'dialectical materialism' to describe this universal method. Carver suggests that Marx was sceptical of such an historical, all-embracing methodology. And there is further supporting evidence for this view (as presented by Lucio Colletti in the Penguin edition of the *Early Writings*) that is not cited by Carver. In addition, Carver is actually silent on the phrase 'dialectical materialism' and the interesting question of its derivation.

In the main this is a work for Marxologists. But its studious iconoclasm should enhance its appeal to a wider audience. One of its rewards is the feeling that the reader has got closer to the texture and dynamic of their thoughts, destroying the myth of an extremely close and interlocking partnership in the process.

On a final point, just as Marx comes through primarily as an economist, it is also possible to credit him with some political sense as well. Carver writes (p29):

> 'Some "extreme socialists", according to Marx, took the lofty view that discussion of current political issues, such as representation in government, was entirely beneath them. . . . Marx's method was to take "*real* struggles" and then to engage in criticism, rather than to follow the dogmatic method practised by communists and socialists when they pronounced their principles and then stated, in Marx's dramatised account: "Here is the truth, kneel down before it!"'

I wonder if Marx was around on the British political scene today he would have a profound sense of *déja vu*?

Geoff Hodgson

Well Fed?

Gluttons for Punishment, by James Erlichman, London, Penguin Books, £2.95.

I suppose one of the greatest obscenities of our age has been the twin image of the dessicated and dying millions of East Africa and Ethiopia set against the food mountains of the Common Market. Obscenity gives way to irony when we remember just how these mountains have been brought about. We are, collectively, paying hundreds of millions of pounds in world terms to the drug companies to pump chemicals, antibiotics and synthetic hormones into animals and spread our fields with unnecessary and harmful pesticides so that we may produce a surplus of food destined for destruction. Obscene, ironic, and also, as it happens, dangerous. This new Penguin, *Gluttons for Punishment*, by James Erlichman, shows us just why.

Greed, as always, is at the bottom of it. This most basic "production for use" industry has now been turned into yet another business, and like any other business, is measured by its balance sheets and not by the numbers it has fed. To the farmer, his accountant, his computerised single animal diet sheets, and his drug pusher are more important than his stockman. He may make more by producing for destruction than for the market. A story from recent weeks: when an eager young Dutch researcher described how they had developed a cure for mastitis, a debilitating cattle disease, the nearest journalist clutched his head and cried despairingly: "Not more milk, please! Not more milk!"

The final irony is that the food itself is now being polluted by the very methods used to produce that surplus. It is almost as if science was being harnessed in the interests of expediting the mythical role of the lemmings. Take that attractive looking supermarket fruit, for example. One major supplier sprays his orchards a dozen separate times before picking. Fruit put into store to await a higher market price is then coated — like a toffee apple! — with a fungicide to prevent rotting. Other fruit and vegetables are often treated to make sure they are properly "cosmetic" on the supermarket shelves. So a whole generation of consumers are being trained by the market to look for precisely the wrong qualities. Nor are the additives necessarily removed by washing. Some are. Others, like DDT, can linger on for years in the food chain. The drive for production by the processors and the drug companies and then consequently the farmers is such that governments are slow to act. After all, the Ministry of Agriculture sees its primary role as promoting the farmer.

There were three lessons to be learned from a fruit incident in California in 1985. The crop involved was water melon, a fruit protected, one would have thought, by the safest and toughest of rinds. Yet, after a hundred cases of nausea and tremors and diarrhoea, the source was identified as watermelon. Ten million, one third of the entire US crop, had to be destroyed. The chemical involved proved to be Aldicarb, a pesticide, says Erlichman, so toxic that "it ranks among the fifteen classified as 'poisonous'." It also happened to be produced by Union Carbide, and the incident happened only months after the disaster at their factory in Bhopal in India. Aldicarb was banned for fruit, but permitted on cotton. Farmers blamed the company — the Aldicarb had lingered on in former cotton fields. The company claimed that the farmers were responsible for "misapplication" of the pesticide.

Company or farmer, a third of the hardest skinned fruit we've got had to be destroyed — lesson one.

Lesson two, probably only the massive events at Bhopal had moved the company and the US Agriculture Department to act.

And lesson three is that Aldicarb is still permitted for use in Britain. There is a number of major anxieties. One, that toxics can move into the food chain and continue to contaminate. Secondly, their continual use can breed resistant strains of bacteria. A major disaster could flow from this. Thirdly, the drive for rapid and exceptional growth in livestock, with weight addition carefully monitored in terms of amount and time, has led to a careless use of growth hormones and antibiotics. Now some of this takes time to show its effects. Clearly there is a grossly insufficient monitoring of this in animals as compared to humans. Yet even with humans, after years of testing of drugs like Thalidomide or Opren, we still ran into major tragedies. The diffusion of drugs in use with animals and throughout the food chain makes the problem of monitoring consequences on human beings after long use a major problem.

All of the pressure for increased production makes farmers put pressure in turn upon their suppliers — and often upon their vets. Most would say they just couldn't afford not to use drugs.

The rise of contract farming has increased this pressure. Often farmers under supply contract to supermarkets or food processors are specifically told which hormones or antibiotics to use. The whole production is then geared to shelf requirements — in appearance, in speed of weight addition, or to be ready for the most marketable date.

Yet as Sainsbury's themselves say,

"Retailers are no more geared up than is Government to continually monitor potential chemical residues in food. At Sainsbury's we have approximately 3,000 own-label food and drink lines alone, from over 700 sources worldwide, distributed in considerable tonnages. Against this background it would be totally impractical in any meaningful way to monitor residues continually."

Yet the whole set-up is not only dangerous but stupid. We are now perfectly capable of feeding ourselves in the West without the enormous damage we are doing to the environment or potentially — and actually — to our own health. The massive energy input into agriculture is at an enormous cost in resources. These produce surpluses which create consequent economic, political and agricultural crises. The surpluses are either stored or destroyed at considerable further cost or, occasionally, shipped inefficiently to a convenient disaster area. Yet these wasted resources could be used to provide the means whereby the third world could feed itself without the destruction of its own basic cultural and agricultural patterns. For those peoples too have been subject to the laws of Western greed. The "green revolution" was itself crippled by the production of new seed that required fertiliser, pesticides, fungicides — provided by the big food and drug multinationals. Erlichman lists a number of steps we should now take. They boil down to the need to know — an end to the commercially based secrecy; the introduction of many more statutory controls; and the extension of monitoring. But above all, we need to put food for healthy consumption before the need for profit of the companies, and therefore the forced interest of farmers.

Perhaps as a first symbolic step we could change the name of the Ministry. Instead of Agriculture, Fisheries and Food, it should simply become Food. I proposed that when I was Minister of State there. It didn't happen. At least it would serve as a permanent reminder to the Ministry of what the primary purpose of agriculture is all about — and it's not to serve the interests and aims of the drug companies.

Norman Buchan MP

Bibliography

Selected Bibliography of Contemporary Strategic Issues, Charles W. Marshall (edited by Kathleen Scott), University of Guelph, Canada

A most useful bibliography on strategic arms, and the attempts to limit them. It ranges from the talks which produced SALT I and II through to the development of the Strategic Defence Initiative, or Star Wars. It has sections on the arms race, and the involvement of the United States, NATO and the Soviet Union. There is a fairly disappointing section on the peace movement.

CK

Conversion

From Swords to Ploughshares — The Conversion of the Belgium Arms Industry, by Bart Buekens, Nico Vanduffel, and Ernst Gulcher, 105pp., 350 Belgian Francs*

This is a report published by the Flemish Peace University under the auspices of the Peace Consultation Centre (Overlegcentrum voor de Vrede — OCV), and in co-operation with the Action Committee Against the Arms Trade-Conversion of the Arms Industry. It addresses itself to all those concerned with this issue, both in Belgium and outside, and in particular to the labour movement. It demonstrates the necessity for and concrete possibilities of converting the Belgian armaments industry to peaceful purposes.

The report is intended to complement studies carried out in other countries on the same subject. It also provides the first Belgian response to the United Nations' challenge that the problems of the arms trade and the militarisation of industry be tackled at a national level.

The study is divided into three sections:

I A general overview of the Belgian armaments industry and the possibilities for conversion;

II A closer look at the Belgian aeronautics firm SABCA, considering the problem of military industries from the point of view of both the Belgian military establishment and the industry's workers;

III A concrete approach to alternative possibilities for Belgian firms that currently produce weapons. Several industrial alternatives are described, as well as the conditions necessary for their success. This section is important for all those who are not familiar with the armaments industry on a day-to-day basis. It considers the possibilities for comprehensive conversion of the industry in the context of the need to extend socially useful but undervalued industrial sectors such as environmental protection, public transport, development assistance and co-operation, and economic collaboration with countries of the Eastern bloc.

Rebecca Gumbrell McCormick

*Available in the Dutch language only under the title *Van Zwaarden Tot Ploegijzers* from the Flemish Peace University (Vlaamse Vredesuniversiteit), Guinardstraat 8, 9000 Ghent, Belgium.

Ending Apartheid

Mark A. Uhliq: *Apartheid in Crisis*, Penguin, 1986, £3.95

This is a curious collection, mostly revised reprints of articles and speeches, which nevertheless contains some interesting and useful material. It is presumably aimed primarily at an American lay audience, and claims to cover "both sides of the political fence".

Thus, there are heartfelt pieces from two South African novelists, Nadine Gordimer and Johan Coatzee, a fairly familiar but effective speech from Desmond Tutu, extracts from a parliamentary speech by van Slabbert just before his resignation in February 1986, an interview with Nelson Mandela, and other pieces. The book concludes with a useful history of South Africa's aggression and destabilisation of the region by David Martin and Phyllis Johnson.

On the other side are extracts from speeches by P.W.Botha and A.P.Treuernicht, so there would appear to be a bias to the Left. But on which side do we place the big centrepiece economic chapter by Michael K.Gavin, now on the board of governors of the US Federal Reserve System? (And why choose him of all people, for the only piece on the economy?) The purpose of the chapter is clearly to oppose sanctions, although alternative strategies for ending apartheid are hard to find; and there are two serious errors, frequently made by opponents of sanctions (and uncorrected elsewhere in the book). Gavin claims that there are 1.5 million migrant workers from Botswana, Lesotho, Swaziland, Malawi, and Mozambique, who might be expelled in the event of sanctions (he is a little behind because the regime has since raised the figure twice, to about 3 million foreign workers — there are negligible numbers from other countries). As the *South African Yearbook for 1984* showed 280,000 (with numbers *declining* since), over half from Lesotho, with possibly as many again present illegally, it is clear that recent "estimates" are a result of the pretence that the Bantustans are independent foreign countries, and/or that there are many times more illegals than legals. If the latter is true, it is hard to see how they could be expelled after sanctions if they cannot be traced and expelled now.

The other old chestnut is that the West would be put into "a very vulnerable position *vis-a-vis* the Soviet Union as the only major supplier" of certain metals. And "after all, countries trade precisely because each needs the other's products". So much for orthodox trade theory and the law of comparative advantage: in fact the West buys from South Africa because, for example, its coal is about half the cost of that from other sources (partly because of the cheap black labour). We don't *need* South Africa's exports (except possibly platinum), we would merely have to pay more elsewhere.

Performing a similar purpose — but more subtly — is a chapter called "Why Constructive Engagement Failed". In its negative aspect this is an excellent attack on the Reagan/Crocker policies. But what to put in their place? Not comprehensive sanctions, of course, but carefully selected ones, such as denying land rights, and "massive aid programs...to help black South Africans attain better educations..." and better monitoring of the performance of US companies in South Africa.

In short, we are mobilised against apartheid by good descriptive and analytic pieces by Gordimer, Martin and Johnson, and others, but the prescriptions are all kept in safer hands. There are better books, such as *The Scope for Sanctions* by Richard Moorsom (CIIR, 1986), and Joe Hanlon's Penguin on sanctions is expected early next year.

Colin Stoneman

Labour Law

Lord Wedderburn, *The Worker and the Law,* Third Edition, Penguin Books, 1986, pp.1026, £10.00

The Labour movement has enjoyed the benefit of Bill Wedderburn's unrivalled scholarship in the field of Labour Law for well over 20 years. Not only is he an academic lawyer of immense distinction, he is a social scientist and a passionate and radical socialist who has always been ready to place his skills and wisdom at the disposal of the movement. In recent years too, he has conducted the Labour Opposition's case against the Thatcher Government anti-union laws, in the House of Lords, exposing not only the legal counter-revolution embodied in them, but also their ideological foundations. More positively, his advice and input into the crucial task of framing a Labour Party programme for future repeal, amendment, and replacement of the Tory laws will be essential.

His Penguin textbook, *The Worker and the Law*, first appeared in 1965, and has been an indispensable work of reference and teaching ever since that seemingly distant and liberal time. A second edition was made in 1971, to include an account of the Heath Government's Industrial Relations Act. The present, completely revised edition, has to include the further fundamental changes wrought in labour law first by the "Social Contract" legislation of 1974-76, and second, the Thatcher laws of 1980, 1982, and 1984. In addition, as the text makes abundantly clear in case after case, the period since the last edition has been marked by an unprecedented level and audacity in judge-made interpretation and extension of statute law.

So British trade union and industrial relations law, as well as law relating to individual employment contract and relationship, have undergone three sweeping sets of revision in the space of 15 years. The principle of legal abstention in labour law, never fully observed in its heyday, has been succeeded by a complex, ever-extending legal network, which absolutely requires minds of the clarity and quality of Bill Wedderburn's, to assist us through its mazes.

The new edition can be unreservedly recommended as an essential possession of all trade unionists, teachers, and students of trade unionism and industrial relations, law students, and would-be legislators. As a reference book, it is fully comprehensive, ranging through individual employment law, job security and dismissal, collective bargaining and the law, statutory provision on wages, hours, and safety, social discrimination at work (sex and race), the law on strikes, the legal relationship between unions and members, and the wider debate on workers' rights. Full tables of statutes and cases are included, as is a well-compiled Index, essential in a work of this kind.

But it should not be thought of solely as a work of reference and information. Throughout, the author sets his account of the changing legal system in its socio-political context, never avoiding his own commitments and feelings, which enhance rather than detract from the book's stature. For, as he writes in his new Preface:

> "Technical law by itself is of limited use, at best an arid game played by keen minds in court rooms and ivory towers. For its significance we need to look at the historical and social setting, to question the values and policies enshrined in the judgments and legal rules, and to enquire into what is done in other countries about the problems revealed."

The browser in the bookshop, if still hesitating over whether to buy this book, is recommended to turn to pages 730 to 744, to discover how powerfully these principles are applied in the text. There will be found an account of the NUM's recent experiences at the hands of the law, the police, and the judges, which is breathtaking for its technical completeness, its measured but committed judgments, and its humane compassion for the suffering of the miners, their families, and communities. In addition, the "climate of opinion" as influenced by prejudice, by politicians and hysterical media, is called in to complete the explanation of judges' attitudes during those bewildering days of 1984-5. Those 14 pages constitute a quite masterly essay in their own right.

The book has over 1,000 pages and is priced at £10.00, which makes it remarkably cheap by today's standards. It is up-to-date to 1st March 1986. The message is simple: buy it!

Tony Topham

THE BERTRAND RUSSELL PEACE FOUNDATION

THE LONDON BULLETIN

Winter 1986-87   **Number 59**

After Reykjavik

AN APPEAL

Following the failure of the Gorbachev-Reagan summit, an appeal was launched at a large demonstration in Rome on 25th October 1986.

"The collapse of the Reykjavik summit meeting, now that details of its exchanges are leaking out, can be seen to offer Europe a warning, but also to offer a hope.

Europeans are not present at these great power negotiations, even though it is our security and our future which are being decided there. We have been deeply concerned about the presence of the intermediate range missiles which are stationed in Europe. Cruise and Pershing on one side, and SS20s on the other, render lethal the divide which cuts our continent in two. In Iceland a preliminary solution was found which could have enabled all such weapons to be dismantled. This solution must be implemented. It must not be lost in a linkage with other questions. Just because we are excluded from the conference rooms, the people of Europe must make their wishes felt on the streets and in the lobbies, to insist on this first crucial step to wider disarmament. We appeal to the Soviet peoples for their support for this call.

But at the same time, Europeans share the planet with all its other inhabitants, and cannot avoid the other issues which came to a head in Reykjavik. On the brink of an agreement to cut stockpiles of strategic weapons by half, the talks failed because of President Reagan's insistence on the testing and deployment of space weapons. Reasonable proposals to solve this problem are available, but they require a willingness on the American side to negotiate. This is, at the moment, not evident. Therefore, in all our demonstrations, we call upon the American people to join us in the effort to persuade their President to reconsider the whole disastrous "Star Wars" commitment.

By joining our forces in this way, we may heed the warning of Reykjavik, and begin to realize its hopes."

The Appeal is being circulated by the Bertrand Russell Peace Foundation. The first signatories are:

Austria: Gerhard Jordan (ARGE UFI);

Belgium: Alfons Boesmans MEP; Andre Bogaert (President, VAKA); Robert de Douai (Vice-President, CNAPD); Robert de Gendt (President, OCV); Jaak Vandemeulebroucke MEP;

Czechoslovakia: Zdena Tominova;

Denmark: E.H.Christiansen MEP; Dagmar Fagerholt (No to Nuclear Weapons); Niels Gregersen (No to Nuclear Weapons); Judith Winther (No to Nuclear Weapons);

France: Sylvie Mantrant (CODENE); Claude Bourdet;

Germany: Jo Leinen (Minister of Environment, Saarbrucken); Eva Quistorp (Women for Peace); Gert Weisskirchen MP;

Greece: The Orthodox Bishop Kissamou; Selinou Erenaeos (President of the Orthodox Academy); Michalis Stathopoulos (Rector of Athens University); General G.Koumanakos (Vice President, KEADEA); Michael Peristerakis (Vice-President IPB); Demetrius Konstas (Rector of Athens Pantios School Political Sciences); General Konstantin Konstantinidis; Panagiotis Gasgas (Vice Mayor of Athens City); Christofer Argiropoulos (President of AKE); Eva Kotamanidou (Actress); Vasso Katraki (Engraver, Venice Bienalle Prize Winner); Kostas Filinis MEP; Kostas Kritsinis (Ex Governor of North Greece); Demetrius Kakavelakis (Author, General Secretary of the International Peace Cape, Crete); Manolis Glezos (President of the United Democratic Left — EDA); G. Romeos MEP; Andreas Lendakis (Mayor of Imitos City);

Italy: Luciana Castellina MEP; Jiri Pelikan MEP;

Netherlands: Maarten van Traa (Dutch Labour Party); Jan ter Laak (Pax Christi); Alex de Zwart (Gruppa Doveriga); Mient-Jan Faber (IKV); Walter Bohle (Dutch Labour Party);

Poland: Jan Minchevitz (Polish Freedom and Peace);

Spain: Manuel Bonmarti (International Secretary, UGT); Marchino Camacho (General Secretary, Comisiones Obreras); Antonio Gala (Playwright, former President Platform Civica para la Salipa OTAN); Manuel Garnaho (UGT); Enrique Gomariz (Editor, Tempo Paz); Gerardo Iglesias (Communist Party Leader, President United Left Coalition); Luis Otero (former Army Major, Spokesman Democratic Military Union); Jose Antonio Martin Pallan (Lawyer, President Human Rights Association); Marisa Rodriguez (Secretary, FEPRI); Francisca Sequillo (Senator, President MPDL); Professor Ramon Tamames (Economist, MP United Left); Professor Juan Jose R.Ugarte (Theologian);

*Sweden:*Gunnar Lassinantti (Swedish Labour Movement Peace Forum);

United Kingdom: Richard Balfe MEP; Bob Cryer MEP; Glyn Ford MEP; Win Griffiths MEP; Alf Lomas MEP; Michael McGowan MEP; David Morris MEP; Stanley Newens MEP; Carole Tongue MEP; Sidney Bidwell MP; Robin Cook MP; Eric Heffer MP; Stuart Holland MP; E. Loyden MP; Martin Flannery MP; Bob Clay MP; Richard Caborn MP; Roland Boyes MP; Robin Corbett MP; Michael Meacher MP; William McKelvey MP; Stan Orme MP; Ron Brown MP; Tony Banks MP; David Blunkett (Leader, Sheffield City Council); CND; Ken Coates (BRPF); Peter Crampton (Chair, END); Ken Fleet (BRPF); Mary Kaldor (END Journal); Margaret Morton (General Secretary, Scottish CND); Paul Rogers; Steven Rose (Russell Committee against Chemical Weapons); Tony Topham; Lord Jenkins of Putney; Professor E. Edwards; Lord Hugh Scanlon; Zhores Medvedev; Ron Todd, General Secretary, T & GWU; Raymond Williams; Victor de Waal; Professor Teodor Shanin; Istvan Meszaros; Leslie Christie, Gen Sec. Society of Civil and Public Servants; Julie Christie; Edna Smee; Steven Lukes; Bishop John V. Taylor; Susannah York;

Yugoslavia: Milos Djukic, Vice-President, Yugoslav League for Peace, Independence and Equality of Peoples; Borut Zupan, Yugoslav League for Peace, Independence and Equality of Peoples.

Nuclear-Free Zones

THIRD INTERNATIONAL CONFERENCE OF LOCAL AUTHORITIES

The Third International Conference of Nuclear-free Local Authorities gathered in Perugia from 9th to 12th October 1986. Convened at a time when the wires were buzzing with news of the Reykjavik summit, the Perugia meeting marked out the solid advance of local authority initiatives on a national and international scale.

Within Italy, the Bertrand Russell Italian Centre was able to publish a register of de-nuclearized towns recording the participation of all the regions from Abruzzo to Veneto. 33 authorities had declared themselves to be non-nuclear towns in the region of Umbria alone. But this record was surpassed by Emilia Romagna, with 100 participating townships, Piemonte, with 44, Sicily, with 35, and, top of the list, Tuscany with 116. Nuclear-free resolutions from the Comunes of Venice, Florence, and Bologna, showed a variety of different initiatives. One of the burning issues confronting the new movement concerned its reaction to nuclear power stations, after the accident at Chernobyl.

The same concern was to be heard in delegations from all over Europe.

But the movement has now ceased to be an impromptu affair. Since the first conference was held in Manchester in 1984, and the second in Cordoba in 1985, a formal constitution has been adopted, and four broad aims have been agreed. These are:

(1) To promote the growth of the local authority nuclear-free zone movement, in order to create a world free of nuclear weapons.

(2) To exchange information and experiences.

(3) To co-ordinate work at an international level.

(4) To develop new international nuclear-free zone initiatives and policies.

Evidence of these new initiatives was to be found in the participation, in Perugia, of a delegation from New Zealand, and of spokesmen and women from the American nuclear-free towns. Larry Ross, an old associate of the Russell Foundation, represented the New Zealand Nuclear-free Zone Committee, of which he is the General Secretary. He was able to report on the developing struggle in New Zealand to remove nuclear weapons from the surrounding zone, and to prohibit them in the entire territory of the country itself. The high point in this campaign was reached with the tabling of the Nuclear Free Zone, Disarmament, and Arms Control Bill in the New Zealand Parliament. We feature the full text of this Bill, in the section which follows.

From the United States, the representative of the State of Chicago was able to report on the adoption of an ordinance establishing Chicago as a nuclear weapon-free zone. We also feature the text of this measure.

Finally, we include the text of the political statements which were approved by the conference.

The Italian Bertrand Russell Centre convened a public meeting to launch its first book, on the idea of nuclear-free zones. Speakers included Luciana Castellina, Ken Coates, and Bill Arkin, of the Institute for Policy Studies. Bill Arkin's paper, on Nuclear Free Zones in Relation to the New Arms Race on Earth and in Space introduces this section in our reports from Perugia.

NFZs and the New Arms Race
William M. Arkin

The United States has more than 500 nuclear weapons on Italian soil. Hundreds more warheads are at sea with the Sixth Fleet, supported by the American and NATO bases in Italy. Italy thus hosts the third largest number of American nuclear weapons outside of the United States — after West Germany and Britain.

One would think from the size of these nuclear deployments that Italy borders a menacing and hostile enemy. But it does not. One would think that it is at the centre of NATO planning for the defence of Europe. It is not. One might conclude that Italy is a close political confidant of the United States. But it is not. Not knowing better, one might guess that the Italian Government is a critical partner with the United States in formulating defence policy and war plans. But it is not.

In fact, read any 10 books by nuclear strategists and you find no mention of Italy at all.

So when one thinks about nuclear weapons in Italy and alternatives to those weapons such as nuclear-free zones, one should not be fooled by what appears to be real, but is not. One should not be fooled by the experts. Self serving military analysts may describe Italy as playing an important defensive role for NATO. But it does not. Italy is isolated from NATO's main focus of attention, which is the central region in West Germany. When it comes to pure military defence against an Army that might be intent on conquest, Italy is easily defensible in the north.

The common public understanding of the reasons for the presence of atomic weapons in Italy — that they serve to deter such an attack — is therefore incorrect. So, the question to be asked is: why all the nuclear weapons, the American bases, and such a large NATO establishment?

Before I answer this question, it is vital to understand what is the precise nature of the nuclear weapons in Italy. This is because not all nuclear weapons are alike. They are different by virtue of where they are and by which service or command of the military controls them. They vary in the ways they can be delivered to the enemy, in how far they can be shot, in how accurate they are, and in what damage they can cause. In 1986, we find ourselves in the situation where military and nuclear strategists have so indulged in diversifying the types and capabilities of their nuclear weapons, they have made the explanations and justifications for them increasingly arcane and convoluted.

Essentially, there are three different kinds of nuclear weapons in Italy; different because they are intended for distinct military roles. The first kind are the nuclear weapons intended for defending against a land invasion. The second are those reserved for a naval nuclear confrontation in the Mediterranean. The third are those of longer range and greater flexibility, eyed by military planners for attacks on the Soviet homeland or for use in contingencies outside Europe.

The first role — land warfare in north-east Italy — is stagnant, obsolete, and ridiculous. Nuclear weapons deployed in northern Italy are a thoughtless continuation of military deployments made in the earliest days of NATO. These nuclear weapons — Lance and Nike Hercules short-range missiles and nuclear artillery projectiles — are unnecessary to defend against, or deter, a land attack which might come across Austria or Yugoslavia.

Even the Reagan Administration understands how absurd these deployments are. They have unilaterally withdrawn nuclear landmines from Longare, near Vicenza, and are reducing the number of nuclear air defence missiles operated by the Italian Air Force. At the same time, recognizing that combat is unlikely in this region, the American parachute battalion in Vicenza has been integrated into the rapid deployment force for the Middle East. This American unit in Italy will most likely be the first military unit available for intervention in North Africa or the Middle East. No one can any longer conceive of a role for this military unit that is relevant to its presence in Italy, other than its proximity to the Middle East.

The second role of American nuclear forces in Italy is supporting the Sixth Fleet and naval warfare in the Mediterranean. For this purpose, anti-submarine nuclear depth bombs and missiles are stored at Sigonella in Sicily and La Maddalena in Sardinia, while Gaeta, Naples, and Sigonella service and support ships and aircraft carriers of the Sixth Fleet.

The naval nuclear role is neither stagnant, harmless, nor ridiculous. Under the Reagan Administration, naval forces have become the primary means to provoke and confront the Soviet Union. The new policy of securing maritime superiority has raised the importance of the Mediterranean in US military planning, because it is here that the largest peacetime concentration of naval units from both countries congregate.

Recent events, such as the deployment of US Marines to Lebanon, the Achille Lauro affair, and the bombing of Libya, all demonstrate a shifting priority and focus towards North Africa and the Middle East for the naval establishment in Italy as well. Given the poor state of US-Greek relations, and overt Turkish sensitivities to being too closely linked with any pro-Israeli policies, the United States finds Italy the most suitable headquarters for Middle East military operations.

The third role of nuclear weapons in Italy and the Mediterranean is also the one which is experiencing the largest growth. This is the nuclear forces which can be flexibly targeted to carry out long-range strikes against the Soviet Union or other countries.

In addition to the aircraft carriers which have been with the Sixth Fleet for decades, we are now witnessing the build-up of ground-launched cruise missiles at Sigonella and Comiso, the introduction of Tomahawk sea-launched cruise missiles aboard attack submarines serviced at La Maddalena, and the deployment of improved Tornado and F-16 aircraft which are nuclear armed at Aviano, Rimini, and Gheddi-Torre. By the end of the decade, some 400 long-range nuclear warheads will be supported by Italian bases.

These long-range weapons are the most dangerous. They transform the military establishment on Italian soil from a defensive force serving a theoretical deterrent function, into a flexible nuclear warfighting force increasingly capable of taking part in strategic attacks on the Soviet Union. Weapons on Italian soil can threaten potential targets inside the Soviet Union for the first time since Jupiter missiles were withdrawn from Gioia Del Colle in the early 1960s.

Aircraft and cruise missiles, in addition, can also be pointed at North Africa and the Middle East. So military planners now have new weapons at their disposal for the occasions when they look over the shoulders to the south.

For so many years, the central front in West Germany has been the attention of European and American military experts. But they do not believe that the Soviet Union is intent on invasion. Governmental and non-governmental military experts believe that if a war occurs at all, it will be because of escalation from a Middle East conflict or a naval confrontation.

Here, in Italy, in the Mediterranean, is where such a risk of war exists. And what has NATO been doing? Building up the naval nuclear forces, air forces and cruise missiles, creating the warfighting flexibility required to prevail in a future conflict, and revising its plans for NATO operations outside its traditional boundaries.

So, when the question is asked: why are there so many nuclear weapons, American bases, and such a large NATO establishment in Italy, it should be clear what the answer is. They are not here merely to deter an invasion, not only to prevent war. They are here to prepare for war, to be used, to fight, to win. The complete answer is kept intentionally hidden.

In the face of growing dissatisfaction with nuclear deterrence, the nuclear priesthood assure us that nuclear weapons are around solely for deterrence. They refuse to acknowledge, to themselves, or to the public, that warfighting has become the norm, or that preparations for war have far outstripped the measures being taken for prevention.

The breakdown of the nuclear consensus has given rise to what today has become the most important reason for the existence and the continuation of the nuclear madness: political solidarity and allegiance to the status quo. Questions dealing with withdrawal from the nuclear addiction are seen, first and foremost, as political heresy. The process of denuclearization carries with it threatening political connotations for the nonconformist. As we have seen with New Zealand, or Greece, or the Netherlands, or Spain, or Denmark, or Norway, or tiny Palau, to question the nuclear rules is to question the Almighty. But again, we shouldn't fool ourselves into thinking that the issue is military.

In the United States, and particularly among the so-called strategic experts, one hears nothing but scepticism about nuclear-free zones. After all, "aren't they just symbolic?", they ask. "Wouldn't nuclear restrictions make it impossible to protect the countries under the nuclear umbrella?", they ask. "Wouldn't businesses who do work relating to nuclear weapons be closed down?", they warn.

The experts have all the answers why any change in the status quo is impossible. But they are wrong. They have deceived the public by creating a handful of nuclear-free zones in areas of the world where they have no interests, and then have used those meagre accomplishments as proof that they are on top of the situation.

But when independent initiatives arise in other places which might actually restrict nuclear war preparations and war games, or reform the system of political conformity to the nuclear idol, new proposals are treated with derision and contempt. And when governments smell an opportunity for expansion of the arms race, as they are now doing with their interest in Star Wars and space, they are prepared to cancel or ignore any treaties which might stand in their way.

The failure of the experts' arms control process, to either control arms or reduce the risk of nuclear war, has given rise to a worldwide movement in favour of independent actions. Villages, municipalities, states, countries, and regions are declaring themselves nuclear-free and imploring the nuclear powers to respect their desire to be the masters of their own destiny. The work in favour of nuclear-weapons-free zones has been a direct expression of public exasperation and rejection. It has become one of the sole means for the local community to register dissent.

The nuclear-free zone movement is so inspiring because it is based on common sense and intuition. Nuclear weapons are bad for you. Nuclear weapons are a threat and a danger. Nuclear secrecy is self-serving and anti-democratic. And the experts and governments shouldn't dispute these points.

Pacific nations have listened patiently for years to the scientific reassurances of governments about the safety of nuclear tests, and to the shrill briefings on the threats and the gaps represented by the evil empire. But the people have concluded that New Zealand, and the South Pacific, should be nuclear-free.

If there are other countries and regions that do not join in on those same anti-nuclear sentiments, it is because they are hostage to the nuclear facilities on their soil, facilities which form an important part of their economic or political lifeblood. Although Italy may be a larger country with diverse resources, it is a nuclear hostage as well.

A common factor in all of the nuclear weapons in Italy, is that, with the exception of the ground-launched cruise missiles, none of them are the subject of any arms control negotiations. Nuclear artillery, naval depth bombs, anti-submarine missiles, Lance missiles, sea-launched cruise missiles, nuclear bombs for tactical jets — none of these weapons are even being discussed for their potential elimination.

What is the reason for such gaps in arms control? It is because arms control is not about the elimination of nuclear weapons, it is about "stability". Stability can be defined as a perpetual attempt to maintain safety in an arms race where constant modernization of nuclear arsenals is required.

Italy is thus hostage to a falsehood: that arms control is arms control. It is not. It doesn't seem capable of controlling anything. Arms control is not even reducing the risk of nuclear war. There are no specific proposals for how to reduce the dangers of confrontation and escalation. If you compare the process of arms control to avoiding car accidents, you would have to conclude that arms control is not a process of driving more carefully; it is, instead, a process of reading about driving more carefully.

The ultimate argument which clever politicians make against nuclear-free zones, or any attempts to upset the nuclear status quo, is that by participating in the nuclear game they have a seat at the table, that they have influenced by participating. But the Italian Government has become a co-operative vassal of the United States in ceding its sovereignty to a nuclear infrastructure which it does interfere with and does not control. Italian soil is used as the springboard for US military intervention in the Arab world. In addition, it has become an suitable and unquestioning nuclear warehouse. Since the Spanish Government restricts nuclear weapons on its soil, nuclear weapons which are needed to support US Air Force fighter planes stationed in Spain are stored in Italy instead. The degree to which political leaders are unfamiliar with military plans and objectives, or the details of their own nuclear predicament, leads me to conclude that a seat at the table has already proven useless.

The most frightening example of the lack of understanding and involvement by nuclear allies is seen in a total abrogation of responsibility over the nuclear infrastructure — that is, the diverse facilities which go into supporting nuclear weapons. Beyond military forces, which are largely visible, there are a multitude of surveillance, communications, command and control, maintenance, and logistic functions which support nuclear warmaking. These facilities, which are more invisible in their functions, form the foundation of military flexibility.

Anti-nuclear and nuclear-free zone movements must take into consideration restrictions on the entire infrastructure. It is not enough today to merely have a physical absence of nuclear warheads.

Improvements in nuclear arsenals and shifts in military strategy ultimately have their biggest impact in peacetime. It is therefore necessary that the military establishments in countries allied to the nuclear powers be re-examined with their expanded roles in mind. While much of nuclear force can be dismissed as merely obsolete and wasteful, much of it is also highly flexible and capable. Ultimately, since the primary concern is peacetime mistakes, or miscalculations, or accidents, nuclear-free zones truly can play a role in reducing the risks of war.

The work in favour of building a non-nuclear world should not be deterred by the conformity and lack of creativity and progress which currently plagues governmental action and arms control.

The Nuclear-Free New Zealand Bill
This is the text of the New Zealand Nuclear Free Zone, Disarmament, and Arms Control Bill introduced into the New Zealand Parliament.

A Bill entitled: An Act to establish in New Zealand a Nuclear Free

Zone, to promote and encourage an active and effective contribution by New Zealand to the essential process of disarmament and international arms control, and to implement in New Zealand the following treaties:

(a) The South Pacific Nuclear Free Zone Treaty of 6th August 1985 (text of which is set out in the First Schedule to this Act):

(b) The Treaty Banning Nuclear Weapon Tests in the Atmosphere, in Outer Space and Under Water of 5th August 1963 (the text of which is set out in the Second Schedule to this Act):

(c) The Treaty on the Non-Proliferation of Nuclear Weapons of 1st July 1968 (the text of which is set out in the Third Schedule to this Act):

(d) The Treaty on the Non-Proliferation of the Emplacement of Nuclear Weapons and other Weapons of Mass Destruction on the seabed and the seafloor and in the subsoil thereof of 11th February 1971 (the text of which is set out in the Fourth Schedule to this Act):

(e) The Convention on the Prohibition of the Development, Production and Stockpiling of Bacteriological (Biological) and Toxin Weapons, and on their Destruction, of 10th April 1972 (the text of which is set out in the Fifth Schedule of this Act):

Be it enacted by the General Assembly of New Zealand in Parliament assembled, and by the authority of the same, as follows:

1. Short Title:— This Act may be cited as the New Zealand Nuclear Free Zone, Disarmament, and Arms Control Act, 1985.

2. Interpretation:— In this Act, unless the context otherwise requires:—

"Biological weapon" means any microbial, or biological agent, or toxin, designed for use as a weapon in armed conflict or for other hostile purposes; and includes equipment designed to facilitate such use:

"Distress" includes force majeure, emergencies, or extreme weather conditions:

"Foreign military aircraft" means any aircraft as defined in section 2 of the Defence Act, 1971, which is for the time being engaged in the service of or subject to the authority or direction of the military authorities of any state other than New Zealand:

"Foreign warship" means any ship, as defined in section 2 of the Defence Act, 1971, which:—

(a) Belongs to the armed forces of a state other than New Zealand, and:—

(b) Bears the external marks that distinguishes ships of that states nationality, and:—

(c) Is under the command of an officer duly commissioned by the government of that state, and:—

(d) Is manned by a crew under regular armed forces discipline:

"Internal waters of New Zealand" means the internal waters of new Zealand as defined by section 4 of the Territorial Sea and Exclusive Economic Zone Act, 1977:

"Nuclear explosive device" means any nuclear weapon or other explosive device capable of releasing nuclear energy, irrespective of the purpose for which it could be used, whether assembled, partly assembled, or unassembled; but does not include the means of transport or delivery of such a weapon or device if separable from and not an indivisible part of it:

"Passage" means continuous and expeditious navigation without stopping or anchoring, except as much as there are, incidental to ordinary navigation, or are rendered necessary by distress or for the purpose of rendering assistance to persons, ships, or aircraft in distress:

"Territorial sea of New Zealand" means the territorial sea of New Zealand as defined by section 3 of the Territorial Sea and Exclusive Economic Zone Act, 1977.

3. Act to bind the Crown:— This Act shall bind the Crown:—

4. New Zealand Nuclear Free Zone:— There is hereby established the New Zealand Nuclear Free Zone, which shall comprise:—

(a) All the land, territory, and inland waters within the territorial limits of New Zealand, and:—

(b) The internal waters of New Zealand; and

(c) The territorial sea of New Zealand, and:—

(d) The airspace above the areas specified in paragraphs (a) to (c) of this section.

Prohibitions in Relation to Nuclear Explosive Devices and Biological Weapons:—

5. Prohibition on acquisition of nuclear explosive devices:— (1) No person, who is a New Zealand citizen or a person ordinarily resident in New Zealand, shall, within the New Zealand Nuclear Free Zone:—

(a) manufacture, acquire, or possess, or have control over, any nuclear explosive device, or:—

(b) aid, assist or abet any person to manufacture, acquire, or possess, or have control over any nuclear explosive device.

(2) No person, who is a New Zealand citizen or a person ordinarily resident in New Zealand, and who is a servant or agent of the Crown, shall, beyond the New Zealand Nuclear Free Zone:—

(a) Manufacture, acquire, or possess, or have control over, any nuclear explosive device, or:—

(b) Aid, assist, or abet any person to manufacture, acquire, possess, or have control over any nuclear explosive device.

6. Prohibition on stationing of nuclear explosive devices:— No person shall emplant, emplace, transport on land or inland waters, stockpile, store, install, or deploy any nuclear explosive device in the New Zealand Nuclear Free Zone.

7. Prohibition on testing of nuclear explosive devices:—
No person shall test any nuclear explosive device in the New Zealand Nuclear Free Zone.

8. Prohibition of biological weapons:— No person shall

manufacture, station, acquire, or possess, or have control over any biological weapon in the New Zealand Nuclear Free Zone.

9. Entry into internal waters of New Zealand:—

(1) When the Prime Minister is considering whether to grant approval to the entry of foreign warships into the internal waters of New Zealand, the Prime Minister shall have regard to all relevant information and advice that may be available to the Prime Minister, including information and advice concerning the strategic and security interests of New Zealand.

The Prime Minister may only grant approval for the entry into the internal waters of New Zealand by foreign warships if the Prime Minister is satisfied that the warships will not be carrying any nuclear explosive device upon their entry into the internal waters of New Zealand.

10. Landing in New Zealand:— (1) When the Prime Minister is considering whether to grant approval to the landing in New Zealand of foreign military aircraft, the Prime Minister shall have regard to all relevant information and advice that may be available to the Prime Minister, including information and advice concerning the strategic and security interests of New Zealand.

(2) The Prime Minister may only grant approval to the landing in New Zealand by any foreign military aircraft if the Prime Minister is satisfied that the foreign military aircraft will not be carrying any nuclear explosive device when it lands in New Zealand.

(3) Any such approval may relate to a category or class of foreign military aircraft and may be given for such period as is specified in the approval.

11. Visits by nuclear powered ships:— Entry into the internal waters of New Zealand by any ship whose propulsion is wholly or partly dependent on nuclear power is prohibited.

12. Passage through territorial sea and straits:— Nothing in this Act shall apply to or be interpreted as limiting the freedom of:—

(a) Any ship exercising the right of innocent passage (in accordance with international law) through or over any strait used for international navigation, or:—

(b) Any ship or aircraft exercising the right of transit passage (in accordance with international law) through or over any strait used for international navigation, or:—

(c) Any ship or aircraft in distress.

13. Immunities:— Nothing in this Act shall be interpreted as limiting the immunities of:—

(a) Any foreign warship or other government ship operated for non-commercial purposes, or:—

(b) Any foreign military aircraft, or:—

(c) Members of the crew of any ship or aircraft to which paragraph (a) or paragraph (b) of this section applies.

14. Offences and penalties

(1) Every person who commits an offence against this Act, who contravenes, or fails to comply with, any provision of sections 5 to 8 of this Act.

(2) Every person who commits an offence against this Act is liable on conviction on indictment to imprisonment for a term not exceeding 10 years.

15. Consent of the Attorney-General to proceedings in relation to offences — (1) No information shall be laid against any person for:—

(a) An offence against this Act, or:—

(b) The offence of conspiring to commit an offence against this Act, or:—

(c) The offence of attempting to commit an offence against this Act, except with the consent of the Attorney-General:—

Provided that a person alleged to have committed any offence mentioned in this subsection may be arrested, or a warrant for any such person's arrest may be issued and executed, and any such person may be remanded in custody or on bail, not withstanding that the consent of the Attorney-General to the laying of any information for the offence has not been obtained, but no further or other proceedings shall be taken until that consent has been obtained.

(2) The Attorney-General may, before deciding whether or not to give consent under subsection (1) of this section, make such inquiries as the Attorney-General thinks fit.

Public Advisory Committee on Disarmament and Arms Control.

16. Establishment of Public Advisory Committee on Disarmament and Arms Control. There is hereby established a committee, to be called the Public Advisory Committee on Disarmament and Arms Control.

17. Functions and powers of committee — (1) The functions of the committee shall be:—

(a) To advise the Minister of Foreign Affairs on such aspects of disarmament and arms control matters as it thinks fit:

(b) To advise the Prime Minister on the implementation of this Act:

(c) To publish from time to time public reports in relation to disarmament and arms control matters and on the implementation of this Act.

(2) The committee shall have all such powers as are reasonably necessary or expedient to enable it to carry out its functions.

18. Membership of Committee:— (1) The Committee shall consist of seven members, of whom:—

(a) One shall be the Minister for Disarmament and Arms Control, who shall be the chairman, and—

(b) One shall be the Secretary of Foreign Affairs, or another officer of the Ministry of Foreign Affairs, nominated from time to time by the Secretary of Foreign Affairs, and:—

(c) One shall be the Secretary of Defence, or another officer of the Ministry of Defence, nominated from time to time by the Secretary of

Defence, and:—

(d) Four shall be appointed by the Minister of Foreign Affairs.

(3) The functions and powers of the Committee shall not be affected by any vacancy in its membership.

19. Procedure of the Committee:— Subject to any directives given by the Ministry of Foreign Affairs, the Committee may regulate its procedure in such manner as it thinks fit.

20. Remuneration and travelling expenses — The Committee is hereby declared to be a statutory board within the meaning of the Fees and Travelling Allowances Act, 1951.

(2) There shall be paid to the members of the Committee, out of money appropriated by Parliament for the purpose, remuneration by way of fees or allowances, and travelling allowances and expenses, in accordance with the Fees and Travelling Allowances Act, 1951, and the provision of that act shall apply accordingly.

21. Money to be appropriated by Parliament for purposes of this Act:— All fees, salaries, allowances, and other expenditure payable or incurred under or in the administration of this Act shall be payable out of money to be appropriated by Parliament for the purpose.

Amendments to other Acts:—

22. Amendments to the Marine Pollution Act, 1974:— (1) The Marine Pollution Act, 1974 is hereby amended by inserting, after section 21 (as enacted by section 4 of the Marine Pollution Amendment Act 1980), the following section:

"21a. Offence to dump radioactive waste:—

(1) Notwithstanding anything to the contrary in this Act, the persons mentioned in subsection (2) of this section commit an offence if:—

"(a) Any radioactive waste is taken on board any ship or aircraft in New Zealand or in New Zealand waters for the purpose of dumping, or:—

"(b) Any radioactive waste is dumped into New Zealand waters from any ship or aircraft to which this part of this Act applies, or:—

"(c) Any radioactive waste is dumped into the sea from any offshore installation or fixed or floating platform, or other artificial structure to which this part of this Act applies, or:—

"(d) Any radioactive waste is dumped into the sea, other than in New Zealand waters, from any New Zealand ship or home-trade ship or New Zealand aircraft.

"(2) The persons who are guilty of an offence under subsection (1) of this section are as follows:—

"(a) In any case to which paragraph (a), or paragraph (b), or paragraph (d) of that subsection applies, the owner and master of the ship, or (as the case may be) the owner of the aircraft and the person in possession of the aircraft:

"(b) In any case to which paragraph (c) of that sub-section applies, the owner of the offshore installation or fixed or floating platform or other artificial structure and the person having control of its operations.

"(3) For the purposes of this section, radioactive waste means material and substances of any kind, form, or description having a specific radioactivity exceeding 100 kilobecquerels per kilogram and a total radioactivity exceeding 3 kilobecquerels.

"(4) Every person who is guilty of an offence under this section:—

"(a) Is liable on summary conviction to a fine not exceeding $100,000, and:—

"(b) Is also liable to pay such amount as the Court may assess in respect of the expenses and costs that have been incurred, or will be incurred, in removing or cleaning up, or dispersing the waste to which the offence relates.

"(5) Nothing in paragraphs (a), (b), and (d) of section 22 (1) of this Act or in paragraph (a) of section 22 (2) of this Act applies in respect of the dumping of radioactive waste."

(2) Section 22b of the Marine Pollution Act, 1974, (as enacted by section 4 of the Marine Pollution Amendment Act, 1980), is hereby amended by inserting, after subsection (6), the following subsection:

"(6a) Notwithstanding anything in this Act, no permit shall authorise the dumping of radioactive waste (as defined in section 21a (3) of this Act)."

23. Amendment to Diplomatic Privileges and Immunities Act, 1968:— The Diplomatic Privileges and Immunities Act, 1968, is hereby amended by inserting, after section 10, the following section:—

"10a. Privileges and immunities of international inspectors pursuant to disarmament treaties — The Governor-General may, from time to time, by Order in Council, confer on any persons who are appointed as inspectors pursuant to any international agreement on disarmament or arms control all or any of the privileges and immunities specified in the third schedule to this Act."

24. Amendment to Official Information Act, 1982:— The Official Information Act, 1982, is hereby amended by inserting in the first schedule, after the item relating to the Phosphate Commission of New Zealand, the following item:—

"Public Advisory Committee on Disarmament and Arms Control."

Ordinance to Establish the City of Chicago as a Nuclear Weapon Free Zone

WHEREAS, the people of Chicago find that the presence of nuclear weapons facilities within Chicago is in direct conflict with the maintenance of the community's public health, safety, morals, economic well-being, and general welfare; and

WHEREAS, the presence of the nuclear weapons industry in Chicago threatens the development of a stable local economy because the demand for nuclear weapons may decline drastically in the event of an arms control agreement or a freeze or reduction in the United

States Government's nuclear weapons arsenal; and

WHEREAS, the allocation of the City's resources in the form of police, fire, and other municipal services to the nuclear weapons industry diverts the City's limited resources from urgently needed human services such as job training, social services for children, the elderly and disabled, shelter for the homeless, education, affordable housing, health care, public transportation, emergency services and public safety; and

WHEREAS, the allocation of the community's private resources in the form of manufacturing, sales, services, education, research and other forms of productive occupation to the nuclear weapons industry diverts the community's limited resources from urgently needed human services such as job training, social services for children, the elderly and disabled, shelter for the homeless, education, affordable housing, health care, public transportation, emergency services and public safety; and

WHEREAS, the allocation of the community's private resources in the form of manufacturing, sales, services, education, research and other forms of productive occupation to the nuclear weapons industry diverts the community's limited resources from fundamental human needs including food, clothing, shelter, education, health care, transportation, art, philosophy and recreation; and

WHEREAS, the security requirements accompanying the nuclear weapons industry unduly restrict the dissemination of information necessary for the citizens of Chicago to make informed decisions regarding the future of their community, and foster a climate of fear and mistrust; and

WHEREAS, the psychological health of the people of the City of Chicago is threatened by the presence of an industry which could make the City a target of terrorism or a nuclear attack that would cause death and destruction unparalleled in human history; and

WHEREAS, the presence of the nuclear weapons industry in Chicago poses a public health threat to the community by increasing the likelihood that this community will be a target of terrorism or a nuclear attack; and

WHEREAS, the public morality is affronted by the presence of an industry profiting from activities which may ultimately lead to unprecedented death and destruction in this community; and

WHEREAS, the people of the City of Chicago clearly expressed their will in 1982 when they passed the Nuclear Weapons Freeze referendum by an overwhelming majority, demonstrating their concern about the issue of nuclear weapons development; and

WHEREAS, the issue of the presence of the nuclear weapons industry in the City has caused severe dissention and discord and has incited its citizens to voice their opposition and to assemble in opposition to such controversial work, and these activities have necessitated the reallocation of scarce police and fire department resources from other important tasks to the control and protection of marchers, demonstrators, protestors and speakers, have on occasion been disruptive of the public order, and have required the City to divert its police forces in order to quell such disruptions, all causing the City great expense; and

WHEREAS, by adopting this ordinance, the City Council, on behalf of the citizens of Chicago, reaffirms the City's commitment to peace and prosperity and fulfils the responsibility it has to the citizens of Chicago who supported the Nuclear Weapons Freeze referendum;

BE IT HEREBY ORDAINED BY THE CITY COUNCIL OF THE CITY OF CHICAGO:

SECTION 1: That a new Chapter 202 of the Municipal Code be enacted, entitled "The Nuclear Weapon Free Chicago Ordinance".

202.1 DEFINITIONS

For the purposes of this ordinance, the following definitions shall apply:

a) "Person" means a natural person, as well as a corporation, institution, or other entity, but shall not include the federal government or any agency thereof.

b) "Nuclear weapon" is any device, the purpose of which is use as a weapon, a weapon prototype, or a weapon test device, the intended detonation of which results from the energy released by fission and/or fusion reactions involving atomic nuclei. For the purpose of this ordinance, "nuclear weapon" includes the weapon's guidance and propulsion system and triggering mechanism, i.e., the means of transporting, guiding, propelling, triggering, or detonating the weapon, provided that such means is destroyed or rendered useless in the normal transporting, guiding, propelling, triggering, or detonation of the weapon.

c) "Component of a nuclear weapon" is any device, radioactive or non-radioactive, specifically designed to be installed in and contribute to the operation of a nuclear weapon.

d) "Direct activities of the federal government" shall mean actions of the federal governments or any agency thereof created by statute, but shall exclude sections of independent contractors.

202.2 PROHIBITIONS OF NUCLEAR WEAPONS WORK

a) Phase-Out of Present Activities: No person shall knowingly, within the City of Chicago, design, produce, deploy, launch, maintain, or store nuclear weapons or components of nuclear weapons. This prohibition shall take effect two years after the adoption and publication of this ordinance.

b) Prohibition of Commencement of Nuclear Weapons Work: No

person who is not, as of the effective date of this ordinance, engaged in the design, production, deployment, launching, maintenance or storage of nuclear weapons or components of nuclear weapons, shall, within the City of Chicago, commence any such activities after the effective date of this ordinance.

c) Exclusions: Nothing in this Section shall be construed to prohibit:
   i) any activity not specifically described in this Section;
   ii) basic research;
   iii) any writing or speech devoted to public commentary or debate or other speech protected by the First Amendment of the United States Constitution;
   iv) the research and application of nuclear medicine;
   v) uses of fissionable materials for smoke detectors, light-emitting watches and clocks, and other consumer products; or
   vi) direct activities of the federal government.

202.3 REDIRECTION OF RESOURCES TOWARDS HUMAN NEEDS

The Mayor of the City of Chicago shall propose, and the City Council shall establish, a Chicago Peace Conversion Commission which shall solicit testimony from the public and prepare a detailed plan for the conversion of resources and physical plants to peaceful and productive uses and to develop alternative sources of employment for persons currently employed in the nuclear weapons industry. The Peace Conversion Plan shall be completed within two years of the adoption of this ordinance. The Commission shall issue an interim report on its progress at the end of the first year following the Commission's first meeting. This interim report shall be presented to the City Council and copies shall be made available to the news media for public dissemination.

The Peace Conversion Commission shall consist of seven members appointed by the Mayor of the City of Chicago, with the advice and consent of the City Council. Following the date of a communication from the Mayor advising the Council of his nominations to the Commission, the City Council shall have 60 days to either approve or reject the Mayor's nominees. Should the City Council not act within that period of time, the Mayor's nominees shall be considered to have received the favourable approval of the City Council. The Mayor shall select one member of the Commission to serve as Chairman of the Commission. The Mayor shall provide staff support for the Commission from the City's Department of Economic Development.

202.4 CIVIL DEFENCE

Recognising the futility of civil defence against nuclear war and its ensuing radioactive contamination, the City declares that planning for or participating in civil defence programmes purporting to prepare for nuclear attack is futile and dangerous. Therefore, the City will not participate in any civil defence or population evacuation programme exclusively intended to be implemented upon the outbreak or threatened outbreak of nuclear hostilities.

Nothing in this Section shall be construed to prohibit or limit any other type of civil defence or emergency preparedness programme.

202.5 NUCLEAR WEAPON FREE ZONE COMMEMORATION DAY

In recognition of the first use of nuclear weapons against the Japanese City of Hiroshima in 1945, 6 August shall be declared "Nuclear Weapon Free Zone Commemoration Day" within the City of Chicago. The City shall sponsor an appropriate observation annually on this date. This annual observation shall include a report by the Mayor on the City's activities to enforce this ordinance.

202.6 NUCLEAR WEAPON FREE ZONE SIGNS

The City shall post and maintain appropriate signs at recognized entrances to the City and in City Hall proclaiming the City of Chicago's status as a nuclear weapon free zone. When posted on city streets or on state or federally supported roads entering the City of Chicago, such signs shall conform with the standards set forth in Section 28-44 of the Federal Highway Administration's *Manual on Uniform Traffic Control Devices for Streets and Highways*.

202.7 ENFORCEMENT

Each violation of this ordinance shall be punishable by up to 30 days imprisonment and a $1,000.00 fine. Each day of violation shall be deemed a separate violation.

202.8 SEVERABILITY

If any section, sub-section, paragraph, sentence or word of this ordinance shall be held to be invalid, either on its face or as applied, the invalidity of such provision shall not affect the other sections, sub-sections, paragraphs, sentences or words of this ordinance, and the applications thereof; and to that end the sections, sub-sections, paragraphs, sentences or words of this ordinance shall be deemed to be severable.

SECTION 2: This ordinance shall be in full force and effect from and after its date of passage.

David D. Orr
Alderman, 49th Ward

Bernard J. Hansen
Alderman, 44th Ward

The Perugia Conference — Three Resolutions

I

This Conference confirms that:

Involvement in the international Local Authority Nuclear Free Zone initiative continues to be open to those Local Authorities who are opposed to the deployment, production, storage, and movement of nuclear weapons, and have accordingly, by formal resolution of the Council, or where appropriate by legally binding referendum, declared their area a Nuclear Free Zone.

The Nuclear Free Zone Local Authorities initiative is an independent movement which is an integral part of the general overall struggle in favour of disarmament. As elected representatives of the people we oppose the arms race and seek concrete measures capable of reversing the present trend which is increasing military expenditure and the quality and quantity of nuclear weapons.

In particular, the Conference demands:

(a) the immediate suspension of all nuclear tests;

(b) the suspension of research projects and of experimentation of new weapons in outer space;

(c) the establishment of Nuclear Free Zones, which must be open to verification by international inspections, as a concrete step towards effective confidence building measures and as a direct reversal of the present trend towards rearmament. This would be an important first step toward achieving international nuclear disarmament;

(d) the reduction and dismantling of all nuclear weapons, especially in Europe East and West.

(e) a commencement by Natural Governments of the process of denuclearisation of all seas and harbours.

The Conference considers that nuclear tests:

(a) represent the very basis of the world arms race;

(b) present serious dangers to the health and life of the people in the area where the tests are carried out;

(c) are a cause of pollution and deterioration of the environment of the whole planet;

(d) imply an enormous waste of resources and a perverted use of science.

The Conference:

i) affirms the need for strong pressure on the nuclear powers from people all over the world in order to achieve a total suspension of nuclear tests;

ii) asks Nuclear Free Zone Local Authorities to commit themselves to develop initiatives in whatever forms are appropriate for each country (e.g., popular petitions; resolutions from City Council; appeals to MPs, Euro MPs, Parliaments, Governments: public statements; etc.) in order to support on the 1st June 1987 (Annual

Nuclear Free Zone Day) a day for an international call for the immediate suspension of nuclear tests;

iii) calls for the International Secretariat to consider what appropriate action should be recommended to countries to take on this day.

Moreover the Conference recognises:

1. the existing link between the production and international marketing of nuclear power and the production and proliferation of nuclear weapons;

2. the inherent dangers for the people which the presence of nuclear weapons and nuclear power present whether arising from strategic purposes planned by military doctrines or possible accidents which may occur in consequence of either the activation of weapons systems or the ordinary activity of nuclear power plants.

This Conference calls upon the International Secretariat in each country to give support to those local authorities who have declared their opposition to use of nuclear power for military civil purposes.

In particular, the Conference proposes the following initiatives to those local authorities who wish to take them into consideration:

(a) commitment to a progressive phasing out of the use of nuclear power, to be achieved within the shortest practical period of time in a planned way and compatible with the needs of each country.

(b) campaigning against the inherent dangers posed by the transportation and disposal of spent fuel and nuclear waste by establishing a monitoring and control system promoted by local authorities in order to obtain information which will create the atmosphere which will lead to the removal of such risks.

(c) campaigning for the immediate halting of the European collaboration on fast reactor technology involving Italy, Belgium, West Germany, France and the United Kingdom.

(d) the promotion of
   (a) positive alternatives to nuclear power and
   (b) employment in the expanded non-nuclear sector.

3. that not all Local Authorities have yet defined their attitude to the use of nuclear power for civil purposes and, therefore, this Conference invites such Authorities to open a debate, as soon as possible, to as to come to a decision on this important issue and inform the International Secretariat Committee accordingly.

The Conference firmly believes that disarmament can only be achieved alongside new strategies of development in different parts of the world. The enormous quantity of resources invested in the arms race together with the increased role of the military in technological and scientific research controls the strategic direction of world economy.

This has had a negative effect on the economies of developed countries and directly resulted in less resources for underdeveloped countries which are the majority of humanity.

The Conference calls on NFZ Local Authorities throughout the world to develop initiatives which would help to alleviate this problem. In order to facilitate this process we all call upon NFZ Local Authorities to press their National Governments to ensure that opportunities exist in the laws of their country, for each Local Authority, if they so choose, to fully develop their NFZ programme.

National policies and the relationship between the Great Powers must be influenced by the commitment, enthusiasm and will of all local authorities. Negotiations and meetings, including those presently taking place and those to be held in the future, are essential because they make available the opportunity for dialogue.

However, it is fundamental for the views of the citizens which we represent to be heard and listened to at such meetings. This voice speaks in favour of the establishment of a new concept of security based on disarmament and peaceful co-existence.

II

In order to further the co-ordination of the NFZ activity throughout the world, this Conference:

(1) Agrees that the International Conference shall take place every two years, the next one being in October 1988.

(2) Agrees that in order to achieve the full international impact consideration should be given to the Conference being held in different continents.

(3) Calls upon the International Secretariat Committee, in conjunction with National Co-ordinating bodies, to agree on a number of area meetings in the intervening years between the International Conference which shall have the same aims as the International Conference, but shall look at them on an area basis.

(4) Calls upon the International Secretariat Committee to positively encourage multi-national events in the intervening years and also authorises the Committee to arrange additional International Conferences if the development of international events merit such a Conference.

(5) Calls upon the International Secretariat Committee to encourage all countries to be represented, in some appropriate form, at all Conferences/Area Meetings whether International or Regional.

(6) Establishes an International Secretariat Committee made up by representatives from each National Co-ordinating Body. The Committee will have the power to co-opt representatives from those countries with no Coordinating Bodies.

(7) Agrees that the International Secretariat shall meet twice a year and shall have the following duties:

(a) To call and direct the organization of the International Conference.

(b) To guarantee the exchange of information and material amongst the different countries about NFZ initiatives.

(c) To protect the development of the Nuclear Free Zone movement and assist in the formation of national co-ordinating bodies in each country.

(d) To prepare a progress report of work carried out over the last two years with a proposed programme for the next two years.

(8) Agrees that the Presidency of the International Secretariat Committee shall be the Chairperson of the United Kingdom Steering Committee and the Secretariat shall be based in Manchester.

(9) Agrees that the Vice Presidency shall be the Province of Perugia who shall have special responsibilities for the collation, publication, and the circulation of an information bulletin concerning nuclear free zone initiatives.

(10) Agrees that at subsequent International Conferences:

(a) At least 50% of the Organising Committee shall be women;

(b) At least 50% of the panel of speakers are women;

(c) At least 50% of Chairpersons are women; and

(d) in view of the total male representation in the speaker's panel this year, great effort be given to securing maximum participation of women speakers in the future years.

(e) Local Authorities should endeavour to send delegations consisting of at least 50% women councillors or officers, and where this cannot be achieved immediately, local authorities should endeavour to nominate women active in the peace movement in their own area, and with appropriate expertise, to represent them.

(f) In order to further the development of awareness of the needs and potential of women, all Conferences should timetable in advance adequate space and time within the programme to enable the particular contribution of women in the peace movement to be made, and for women to meet together.

(11) Agrees that appropriate changes be made to the existing condition to facilitate the above proposals.

PROCEDURAL MATTERS
NATIONAL CO-ORDINATING BODIES

(1) This Conference urges all Nuclear Free Zone Local Authorities to consolidate their work and to establish National Co-ordinating bodies where they do not exist.

INTERNATIONAL CONFERENCE 1988

(2) The following Authorities have expressed an interest in hosting the 1988 International NFZ Conference.

Wollongong — Australia

Delft	— Holland
	— Japan
Düsseldorf	— Fed. Rep. Germany
Glasgow	— Scotland
Amsterdam	— Holland
Tacoma Park	— USA

The Conference Committee recommends the following procedure for consideration of these and any other offers.

(a) Any Authority wanting to express an initial interest or wanting details of what would be entailed in hosting the Conference is asked to write, by no later than 31st December 1986 to:
International Secretariat
International NFZ Local Authorities
Manchester City Council
Town Hall
Manchester M60 2LA
England

(b) The International Secretariat will provide these Authorities with a detailed breakdown of facilities needed and costs involved.

(c) If after considering the information provided by the secretariat, an Authority wants to make an official offer, this should be sent to the International Secretariat, in the name of the Mayor, to arrive no later than 30th April 1987.

(d) The International Secretariat Committee will meet before June 30th 1987 to consider the offers made to make their decisions.

III

OMNIBUS RESOLUTION

The omnibus resolution contains the proposals which the International Conference Committee received and which they were able to support for recommendation to Conference.

The vast majority of proposals have been accepted by the Conference Committee. In some cases proposals have been altered or composited in order not to create duplication.

In a small number of cases the Conference Committee was not able to recommend the proposals to Conference for approval.

(1) Conference welcomes and confirms the action of the Chairman of the Conference Organising Committee in writing to Reagan and Gorbachev before their Summit meeting seeking a precise commitment from them in relation to issues contained in the General Political Statement submitted to Conference.

Conference agrees to send a message to Reagan and Gorbachev suggesting that next Summit be held in Hiroshima and recommends all National delegations to issue press releases endorsing this proposal and all NFZ Local Authorities to submit letters along these lines to Reagan and Gorbachev.

(2) This Conference agrees that the following activities should have more priority in the next years:

— To stimulate local authorities in Western Europe to enter into friendship ties with towns in Eastern Europe in order to promote a detente from below.

— To encourage cities in Eastern Europe to attend as observers at the next Conference.

— To develop more elaborate and effective peace education programmes.

— To search for ways in which nuclear free zones could communicate with and influence national governments.

(3) That the International Secretariat Committee apply to the United Nations, before the end of December 1986 (as part of the International Year of Peace) for formal 'Non Governmental Organization' status. That a list of all NFZs in the world be compiled, country by country, and submitted to the United Nations with the application.

(4) That this Conference pledges its full support for the 13 Nuclear Free Zone initiatives that will be voted on this fall in North America — in Hawaii, Ohio, British Columbia, California and Oregon — and especially for the Oregon Nuclear Weapons Conversion Measure, the first statewide, legally-binding, NFZ initiative, which if passed, will require the phase-out of all nuclear weapons work within the state by 1990.

(5) That this Conference petitions the United States Congress to respect the Nuclear Free Constitution of the Republic of Belau in the Pacific Islands *and* to abide by the decision of the Supreme Court of Belau (of 27 August 1986) rejecting the latest "Compact of Free Association" proposed by the United States as unconstitutional.

(6) Conference calls upon those nations upon whose territories exist superpower bases containing high technology facilities used for communications, navigations and surveillance, with the support of the world community, to phase control of such bases away from the controlling power as these facilities enhance the war-making capability of the superpowers.

(7) Conference recognises the valuable role of verification which surveillance bases/facilities could play for peace and it therefore proposes that bases containing such technology should revert to the control of a consortium of nations — e.g. the non-aligned nations, the host nation and all superpowers.

Conference records that it does not oppose the civil use of these communication centres.

(8) This Conference calls on nations currently mining and selling uranium, the basic element which makes possible the constitution of nuclear weapons and the functioning of nuclear establishments which create so much misery to humanity, to plan a sensible reduction of

those activities. In achieving this reduction the requirements of the present irreplaceable needs for nuclear power supply in some countries and primary medical needs are to be taken into consideration.

(9) This Conference calls upon those Local Authorities who are able to do so at this point in time to give full and active support to Scottish Nuclear Free Zone Local Authorities in their efforts to prevent the commissioning of the advanced gas cooled reactors at Torness, East Lothian, and the expansion of Dounreay, Caithness, through the siting there of the European Demonstration Reprocessing Plant for reprocessing spent fast reactor fuel.

Yugoslavia

SOCIALIST ECONOMISTS MEET

For 11 years now, a most interesting forum has been developing at Cavtat in Yugoslavia. "Socialism in the World" is the general heading for a series of wide-ranging seminars, in which a very broad spectrum of socialist opinions are developed, in a free and stimulating discussion. On 20th October 1986, the 11th forum gathered to consider the topic "Socialism and the Economy". The British contingent included Stuart Holland, Michael Barratt Brown, Ken Coates, and David Blunkett, as well as representatives of the British Communist Party and *New Left Review*.

The forum was opened by Dr.Alexander Grlickov, on behalf of its Yugoslav sponsors, the three major socialist theoretical reviews in the country.

From socialist countries papers were submitted on economic development in China and the Soviet Union, and on the problems encountered in Bulgaria, East Germany, Hungary, and Romania. There was a very lively debate among the numerous Yugoslav contingent.

Western economists presenting papers included Paul Sweezy, Harry Magdoff, Ulf Himmelstrand, and Andre Gunder Frank. Samir Amin and Anouar Abdel-Malek were among the distinguished contingent of spokesmen from the non-aligned world.

Colombia

THE CAMPAIGN AGAINST DISAPPEARANCES

Amnesty International has received reports that Silvio Mesa Cortes, a street vendor aged 23, was abducted at about 6.30pm on 12 November 1986 as he was standing in a queue outside a cinema in the city of Cali, in Valle Department. According to these reports, he was seized by heavily armed men in civilian clothes and forced into a car. Although his relatives and local human rights groups have sought information about his whereabouts and the reasons for his detention from the police and military authorities, they have denied that Silvio Mesa Cortes is in detention.

Amnesty International is concerned that Silvio Mesa Cortes may be held in secret, unacknowledged detention in police or military installations in Cali, and that he may be tortured or killed. Amnesty has received frequent reports of "disapearance" and extrajudicial execution from the Valle Department during 1986.

Mr Everth Marin Cortini, aged 29, left his brother's house in Cali at 5pm on 9 October 1986 on his motorbike to do some shopping. He has since not been seen nor has he contacted friends or family, who are extremely worried as to his whereabouts and safety. Fears for Mr Marin's life are well founded as he has been an active member of the Committee for Solidarity with Political Prisoners in Colombia. It is "normal" in Colombia for people involved in Human Rights and similar organisations to be threatened with physical violence, assassination or "disappearance" by the army, police or one of the many death squads who roam the country.

Message to the First International Colloquium on Enforced Disappearances in Colombia.

The tragic agenda of your Colloquium is a challenge to the conscience of humanity, and to the behaviour of all international organizations which are concerned with the issues of human rights. Since the convocation of the Bertrand Russell Tribunal on Repression in Latin America, we have been aware of serious progress in some parts of the continent, with the return to democratic forms of government in some of the most important States of the region. It remains true that there are still serious grounds for concern, and for international action.

Your conference will draw attention to some of the gravest violations of human rights in the contemporary world, and its deliberations, if justice truly prevailed throughout most of the world, would receive priority attention throughout the major world media. We regret to say that, in our experience, this is unlikely to happen. Many of the worst atrocities with which your meeting will be concerned have been virtually ignored by responsible newspapers and broadcasting institutions. Their silence is inexcusable. It deprives the victims of barbarous repression of the one resource to which they have an undeniable right: the moral support and sympathy of concerned people all around the world.

We very much wish we could be with you during these days, but even in our absence, we want to assure you of our wholehearted support. If there is anything we can do to draw the fire of public criticism on those who perpetrate the horrific actions against which you are protesting, we hope you will inform us. Meantime, we offer you our most heartfelt good wishes. Your courage and dedication to human dignity is an example to all of us.

Ken Coates,
Bertrand Russell Peace Foundation

The United Nations

THE FUNDING CRISIS

The United Nations Organization has grown continuously since its formation, as have the variety of specialised agencies working within its general framework. In the earliest years the Organization was under the dominant influence of the powers which were allied during the Second World War. De-colonization, and the collapse of old imperial networks, have steadily expanded the number of independent states presenting themselves for admission, and now the United Nations is almost universal in its inclusiveness and scope. It is also less predictable than it once was, in the decisions it takes.

In recent years, the United Nations has attracted strong criticism from a number of people who have been unhappy about the UN's growing influence in the world, and about the fact that some of its judgements have been uncomfortable for some powers. In the United States in particular, a very wealthy organisation, called the Heritage Foundation, has been campaigning with considerable professional skill to reduce the influence of the UN, and to weaken some of the specialised agencies. Mr Gough Whitlam, the former Prime Minister of Australia, has described the campaign for dis-affiliation from UNESCO, in a paper which gives occasion for some concern, indeed, alarm.

More recently, cuts in the funding of the United Nations Organization have posed very considerable problems for its efficient functioning.

We believe that the United Nations Organization retains a vital importance in the modern world. As the only truly comprehensive international organisation, it necessarily attracts appeals and arouses expectations. Under its Charter, it sustains the International Court of Justice, which nurtures the hopes of civilised people that the world may evolve a truly general system of international law.

The UN suffers from many weaknesses, and could arguably be reformed in a number of beneficial directions. However, if it is to be improved and developed, it must be sustained: to weaken it by undermining its resources is no way to render its operation more efficient, or more equitable.

Because we are worried about the present international situation, fraught with economic crisis and military confrontations, we feel that it is more than ever necessary to support the United Nations. Therefore we join our voices in an appeal to all the governments of Europe. Without prejudice to any needs for future reforms or changes, we urge such governments to join together to guarantee the adequate development of the UN as an Organization. We suggest that each government in Europe should agree to combine with all the others in raising a sufficient sum of money to eliminate any present UN deficits, and that a joint European appeal be launched by the same governments, to organise public subscriptions on a scale large enough to maintain effective international association during forthcoming years. We appeal to public organisations to join us in requesting our governments to consider such action and we appeal to individual Europeans to sign this letter, and give it their active support.

Signed: Archbishop of York, Most Rev. and Rt. Hon. John Habgood; Bishop of Bath and Wells, Rt. Rev. John Bickersteth; Bishop of Chichester, Rt. Rev. Eric Kemp; Former Bishop of Winchester, Rt. Rev. John V. Taylor; Lord Fenner Brockway; Lord Gifford, QC; Lord Jenkins of Putney; Lord Hugh Scanlon; Ron Todd, General Secretary, TGWU; Zhores Medvedev; Raymond Williams; Alan Plater; W.L. Nicholas; Steven Lukes; Bryan Gould MP; Istvan Meszaros; Victor de Waal; Lewis Minkin; Stephen Bodington; Tony Simpson; Tony Topham; Bob Edwards MP; Frank Cook MP; Norman Buchan MP; Dafydd Wigley MP; Tony Benn MP; Clare Short MP; Joan Maynard MP; Roland Boyes MP; Richard Caborn MP; Bob Clay MP; Marisa Rodriguez; Claude Bourdet; Ken Coates; Ken Fleet.

The Sixth END Convention

COVENTRY CHOSEN AS VENUE

The Sixth Convention on European Nuclear Disarmament will assemble in Coventry, England, on Wednesday 15 July 1987, and will meet until Sunday, 19 July in a series of plenary sessions, large and small meetings, and a great variety of workshops and cultural events. Over a thousand participants are expected from all over Europe with visitors from the United States and many Third World countries.

The Convention assembles at a time of crisis in Europe and the wider world. The collapse of the latest superpower summit in Reykjavik, the ever escalating arms race which now threatens the space surrounding our planet and the widening gap between North and South all combine to make the world less secure. The disaster at Chernobyl has heightened fears concerning the entire nuclear fuel cycle.

Europe now faces a choice between continuing to serve the needs of the superpowers, of evolving as a new superpower itself or of developing genuinely novel peace and security policies for its own and the world's survival.

While Europeans confront these questions, Britain enters a general election in which disarmament and security have become central issues. For the first time the people are being offered a real choice between further nuclear aggrandisement or a non-nuclear defence with the promise of a move towards non-provocative defence.

The Convention will provide an open forum for all those concerned with these issues — East and West, North and South. It will pursue broad themes: What kind of Europe are we aiming for, in what kind of world? What type of security policies fit with the process of disarmament and detente? How can the peace movements extend their influence to cope with the challenge posed by militarism? The Convention will also involve a broad cultural programme and many self organised workshops on the widest variety of related issues.

Detailed information about the Programme and Registration available from: Ken Fleet, Bertrand Russell House, Gamble Street, Nottingham NG7 4ET (Telephone: 0602 784504).

Joint Action for Jobs
A New Internationalism

Edited by Ken Coates, with a foreword by Stuart Weir

Unemployment is laying Europe waste. With twenty million people out of work, the number of direct victims has become intolerable: a common scandal. But there is every reason to believe that this number is growing steadily, whilst the direct sufferers already include whole populations. Yet there is no reason to believe that unemployment is unavoidable or fore-ordained. A mere fraction of the ingenuity which has transformed our technical capacities could re-arrange our social rules in a way which would guarantee a useful role for all our people.

Of course, action by Governments can improve or worsen this condition. If all or even some of the European Governments were willing to act together in order to reject mass unemployment, there is no doubt that conditions could be radically improved. But this is not a problem which can be left to governments. Because it concerns everybody, it needs action by all of us. The work which is necessary requires us to find ways of joining needs to resources, of restructuring institutions to regain the democratic initiative in the global economy. We must find ways to replace the policies of 'beggar my neighbour' by those which seek instead to 'better my neighbour'.

"These excellent essays show how vital it is for socialists who wish to have an impact on unemployment to broaden their horizons, and think internationally".

Ben Pimlott

"Reflecting the thought and experience of those who have already been involved in local enterprise, and building networks to transcend national boundaries, it is an important contribution not only to the debate but to the practical answer to the tens of millions of people without jobs and without the prospect of work in the industrialised world".

David Blunkett

". . . a serious attempt to seek an international solution to some of the major economic problems facing the next Labour Government. It is vital for the Labour Party that it be widely discussed.

Lewis Minkin

Paper £4.95
Cloth £17.50
232pp

ISBN 0 85124 428 9
ISBN 0 85124 427 0

SPOKESMAN
Bertrand Russell House, Gamble Street, Nottingham, UK
Tel. 0602 708318